99 POEMS

ALSO BY DANA GIOIA

99 POEMS

New & Selected

. . .

BY

Dana Gioia

Graywolf Press

This publication is made possible, in part, by the voters of Minnesota through a Minnesota State Arts Board Operating Support grant, thanks to a legislative appropriation from the arts and cultural heritage fund, and a grant from the Wells Fargo Foundation. Significant support has also been provided by Target, the McKnight Foundation, the Amazon Literary Partnership, and other generous contributions from foundations, corporations, and individuals. To these organizations and individuals we offer our heartfelt thanks.

Published by Graywolf Press
250 Third Avenue North, Suite 600
Minneapolis, Minnesota 55401

www.graywolfpress.org

Published in the United States of America

ISBN 978-1-55597-732-0 (cloth)
ISBN 978-1-55597-771-9 (paper)

4 6 8 10 11 9 7 5 3

Library of Congress Control Number: 2016938841

Cover design: Kyle G. Hunter

For My Sons

MIKE AND TED

Beloved Sons and Fellow Writers

CONTENTS

I. Mystery

II. Place

III. Remembrance

IV. Imagination

V. Stories

VI. Songs

VII. Love

99 POEMS

· I ·

MYSTERY

THE BURNING LADDER

Jacob

never climbed the ladder
burning in his dream. Sleep
pressed him like a stone
in the dust,

> and when

he should have risen
like a flame to join
that choir, he was sick
of traveling,

> and closed

his eyes to the Seraphim
ascending, unconscious
of the impossible distances
between their steps,

> missed

them mount the brilliant
ladder, slowly disappearing
into the scattered light
between the stars,

> slept

through it all, a stone
upon a stone pillow,
shivering. Gravity
always greater than desire.

INSOMNIA

Now you hear what the house has to say.
Pipes clanking, water running in the dark,
the mortgaged walls shifting in discomfort,
and voices mounting in an endless drone
of small complaints like the sounds of a family
that year by year you've learned how to ignore.

But now you must listen to the things you own,
all that you've worked for these past years,
the murmur of property, of things in disrepair,
the moving parts about to come undone,
and twisting in the sheets remember all
the faces you could not bring yourself to love.

How many voices have escaped you until now,
the venting furnace, the floorboards underfoot,
the steady accusations of the clock
numbering the minutes no one will mark.
The terrible clarity this moment brings,
the useless insight, the unbroken dark.

THE STARS NOW REARRANGE THEMSELVES

The stars now rearrange themselves above you
but to no effect. Tonight,
only for tonight, their powers lapse,
and you must look toward earth. There will be
no comets now, no pointing star
to lead where you know you must go.

Look for smaller signs instead, the fine
disturbances of ordered things when suddenly
the rhythms of your expectation break
and in a moment's pause another world
reveals itself behind the ordinary.

And one small detail out of place will be
enough to let you know: a missing ring,
a breath, a footfall or a sudden breeze,
a crack of light beneath a darkened door.

NOTHING IS LOST

Nothing is lost. Nothing is so small
that it does not return.
                                    Imagine
that as a child on a day like this
you held a newly minted coin and had
the choice of spending it in any way
you wished.
                        Today the coin comes back to you,
the date rubbed out, the ancient mottoes vague,
the portrait covered with the dull shellac
of anything used up, passed on, disposed of
with something else in view, and always worth
a little less each time.
                                Now it returns,
and you will think it unimportant, lose
it in your pocket change as one more thing
that's not worth counting, not worth singling out.
That is the mistake you must avoid today.
You sent it on a journey to yourself.
Now hold it in your hand. Accept it as
the little you have earned today.
                                    And realize
that you must choose again but over less.

DO NOT EXPECT

Do not expect that if your book falls open
to a certain page, that any phrase
you read will make a difference today,
or that the voices you might overhear
when the wind moves through the yellow-green
and golden tent of autumn, speak to you.

Things ripen or go dry. Light plays on the
dark surface of the lake. Each afternoon
your shadow walks beside you on the wall,
and the days stay long and heavy underneath
the distant rumor of the harvest. One
more summer gone,
and one way or another you survive,
dull or regretful, never learning that
nothing is hidden in the obvious
changes of the world, that even the dim
reflection of the sun on tall, dry grass
is more than you will ever understand.

And only briefly then
you touch, you see, you press against
the surface of impenetrable things.

BEWARE OF THINGS IN DUPLICATE

Beware of things in duplicate:
a set of knives, the cufflinks in a drawer,
the dice, the pair of Queens, the eyes
of someone sitting next to you.
Attend that empty minute in the evening
when looking at the clock, you see
its hands are fixed on the same hour
you noticed at your morning coffee.
These are the moments to beware
when there is nothing so familiar
or so close that it cannot betray you:
a twin, an extra key, an echo,
your own reflection in the glass.

ALL SOULS'

Suppose there is no heaven and no hell,
And that the dead can never leave the earth,
That, as the body rots, the soul breaks free,
Weak and disabled in its second birth.

And then invisible, rising to the light,
Each finds a world it cannot touch or hear,
Where colors fade and, if the soul cries out,
The silence stays unbroken in the air.

How flat the ocean seems without its roar,
Without the sting of salt, the bracing gust.
The sunset blurs into a grayish haze.
The morning snowfall is a cloud of dust.

The pines that they revisit have no scent.
They cannot feel the needled forest floor.
Crossing the stream, they watch the current flow
Unbroken as they step down from the shore.

They want their voices to become the wind—
Intangible like them—to match its cry,
Howling in treetops, covering the moon,
Tumbling the storm clouds in a rain-swept sky.

But they are silent as a rising mist,
A smudge of smoke dissolving in the air.
They watch the shadows lengthen on the grass.
The pallor of the rose is their despair.

ON APPROACHING FORTY

The thought pursues me through this dreary town
where the wind sweeps down from the high plateau
and where a diving chimney swift can cut
the slender thread of mountains far away.

So soon come forty years of restlessness,
of tedium, of unexpected joy,
quick as a gust of wind in March is quick
to scatter light and rain. Soon come delays,
snatched from the straining hands of those I love,
torn from my haunts, the customs of my years
suddenly crushed to make me understand.
The tree of sorrow shakes its branches . . .

The years rise like a swarm around my shoulders.
Nothing has been in vain. This is the work
which all complete together and alone,
the living and the dead, to penetrate
the impenetrable world, down open roads,
down mineshafts of discovery and loss,
and learned from many loves or only one,
from father down to son—till all is clear.

And having said this, I can start out now,
easy in the eternal company
of all things living, of all things dead,
to disappear in either dust or fire
if any fire endures beyond its flame.

(From the Italian of Mario Luzi)

MAZE WITHOUT A MINOTAUR

If we could only push these walls
apart, unfold the room the way
a child might take apart a box
and lay it flat upon the floor—
so many corners cleared at last!
Or else could rip away the roof
and stare down at the dirty rooms,
the hallways turning on themselves,
and understand at last their plan—
dark maze without a minotaur,
no monsters but ourselves.
                  Yet who
could bear to see it all? The slow
descending spirals of the dust
against the spotted windowpane,
the sunlight on the yellow lace,
the hoarded wine turned dark and sour,
the photographs, the letters—all
the crowded closets of the heart.

One wants to turn away—and cry
for fire to break out on the stairs
and raze each suffocating room.
But the walls stay, the roof remains
strong and immovable, and we
can only pray that if these rooms
have memories, they are not ours.

WORDS

The world does not need words. It articulates itself
in sunlight, leaves, and shadows. The stones on the path
are no less real for lying uncatalogued and uncounted.
The fluent leaves speak only the dialect of pure being.
The kiss is still fully itself though no words were spoken.

And one word transforms it into something less or other—
illicit, chaste, perfunctory, conjugal, covert.
Even calling it a *kiss* betrays the fluster of hands
glancing the skin or gripping a shoulder, the slow
arching of neck or knee, the silent touching of tongues.

Yet the stones remain less real to those who cannot
name them, or read the mute syllables graven in silica.
To see a red stone is less than seeing it as jasper—
metamorphic quartz, cousin to the flint the Kiowa
carved as arrowheads. To name is to know and remember.

The sunlight needs no praise piercing the rainclouds,
painting the rocks and leaves with light, then dissolving
each lucent droplet back into the clouds that engendered it.
The daylight needs no praise, and so we praise it always—
greater than ourselves and all the airy words we summon.

INTERROGATIONS AT NOON

Just before noon I often hear a voice,
Cool and insistent, whispering in my head.
It is the better man I might have been,
Who chronicles the life I've never led.

He cannot understand what grim mistake
Granted me life but left him still unborn.
He views his wayward brother with regret
And hardly bothers to disguise his scorn.

"Who is the person you pretend to be?"
He asks, "The failed saint, the simpering bore,
The pale connoisseur of spent desire,
The half-hearted hermit eyeing the door?

"You cultivate confusion like a rose
In watery lies too weak to be untrue,
And play the minor figures in the pageant,
Extravagant and empty, that is you."

ENTRANCE

Whoever you are: step out of doors tonight,
Out of the room that lets you feel secure.
Infinity is open to your sight.
Whoever you are.
With eyes that have forgotten how to see
From viewing things already too well-known,
Lift up into the dark a huge, black tree
And put it in the heavens: tall, alone.
And you have made the world and all you see.
It ripens like the words still in your mouth.
And when at last you comprehend its truth,
Then close your eyes and gently set it free.

(From the German of Rainer Maria Rilke)

NEW YEAR'S

Let other mornings honor the miraculous.
Eternity has festivals enough.
This is the feast of our mortality,
The most mundane and human holiday.

On other days we misinterpret time,
Pretending that we live the present moment.
But can this blur, this smudgy in-between,
This tiny fissure where the future drips

Into the past, this flyspeck we call *now*
Be our true habitat? The present is
The leaky palm of water that we skim
From the swift, silent river slipping by.

The new year always brings us what we want
Simply by bringing us along—to see
A calendar with every day uncrossed,
A field of snow without a single footprint.

THE ANGEL WITH THE BROKEN WING

I am the Angel with the Broken Wing,
The one large statue in this quiet room.
The staff finds me too fierce, and so they shut
Faith's ardor in this air-conditioned tomb.

The docents praise my elegant design
Above the chatter of the gallery.
Perhaps I am a masterpiece of sorts—
The perfect emblem of futility.

Mendoza carved me for a country church.
(His name's forgotten now except by me.)
I stood beside a gilded altar where
The hopeless offered God their misery.

I heard their women whispering at my feet—
Prayers for the lost, the dying, and the dead.
Their candles stretched my shadow up the wall,
And I became the hunger that they fed.

I broke my left wing in the Revolution
(Even a saint can savor irony)
When troops were sent to vandalize the chapel.
They hit me once—almost apologetically.

For even the godless feel something in a church,
A twinge of hope, fear? Who knows what it is?
A trembling unaccounted by their laws,
An ancient memory they can't dismiss.

There are so many things I must tell God!
The howling of the damned can't reach so high.
But I stand like a dead thing nailed to a perch,
A crippled saint against a painted sky.

PROPHECY

Sometimes a child will stare out of a window
for a moment or an hour—deciphering
the future from a dusky summer sky.

Does he imagine that some wisp of cloud
reveals the signature of things to come?
Or that the world's a book we learn to translate?

And sometimes a girl stands naked by a mirror
imagining beauty in a stranger's eyes
finding a place where fear leads to desire.

For what is prophecy but the first inkling
of what we ourselves must call into being?
The call need not be large. No voice in thunder.

It's not so much what's spoken as what's heard—
and recognized, of course. The gift is listening
and hearing what is only meant for you.

Life has its mysteries, annunciations,
and some must wear a crown of thorns. I found
my Via Dolorosa in your love.

And sometimes we proceed by prophecy,
or not at all—even if only to know
what destiny requires us to renounce.

O Lord of indirection and ellipses,
ignore our prayers. Deliver us from distraction.
Slow our heartbeat to a cricket's call.

In the green torpor of the afternoon,
bless us with ennui and quietude.
And grant us only what we fear, so that

Underneath the murmur of the wasp
we hear the dry grass bending in the wind
and the spider's silken whisper from its web.

THE ROAD

He sometimes felt that he had missed his life
By being far too busy looking for it.
Searching the distance, he often turned to find
That he had passed some milestone unaware,
And someone else was walking next to him,
First friends, then lovers, now children and a wife.
They were good company—generous, kind,
But equally bewildered to be there.

He noticed then that no one chose the way—
All seemed to drift by some collective will.
The path grew easier with each passing day,
Since it was worn and mostly sloped downhill.
The road ahead seemed hazy in the gloom.
Where was it he had meant to go, and with whom?

PRAYER AT WINTER SOLSTICE

Blessed is the road that keeps us homeless.
Blessed is the mountain that blocks our way.

Blessed are hunger and thirst, loneliness and all forms of desire.
Blessed is the labor that exhausts us without end.

Blessed are the night and the darkness that blind us.
Blessed is the cold that teaches us to feel.

Blessed are the cat, the child, the cricket, and the crow.
Blessed is the hawk devouring the hare.

Blessed are the sinner and the saint who redeem each other.
Blessed are the dead, calm in their perfection.

Blessed is the pain that humbles us.
Blessed is the distance that bars our joy.

Blessed is this shortest day that makes us long for light.
Blessed is the love that in losing we discover.

MONSTER

Night-born, malformed, maleficent,
pale as a pulled root,
a monster prowls the woods.

What other explanation is there
for the gutted deer, the naked
footprint by the bedroom window?

Now the neighbor's dog
has disappeared. The back gate's broken.
I keep the shotgun loaded.

How often now the birds
suddenly go silent in the trees.
What do they hear?

This thing of darkness I
acknowledge mine. I made it.
I let it escape. Now it returns.

Go on, you ragged underling.
Stalk me with your pitiful strategies.
Starve and shiver in the darkness.

Cry to me from the thorny ravine.
I'm safe behind locked doors.
I will not answer or embrace

the thing I have created.

HOMAGE TO SOREN KIERKEGAARD

Work out your own salvation
with fear and trembling.

—ST. PAUL

I was already an old man when I was born.
Small with a curved back, he dragged his leg when walking
the streets of Copenhagen. "Little Kierkegaard,"
they called him. Some meant it kindly. *The more one suffers*
the more one acquires a sense of the comic.
His hair rose in waves six inches above his head.
Save me, O God, from ever becoming sure.
What good is faith if it is not irrational?

Christianity requires a conviction of sin.
As a boy tending sheep on the frozen heath,
his starving father cursed God for his cruelty.
His fortunes changed. He grew rich and married well.
His father knew these blessings were God's punishment.
All would be stripped away. His beautiful wife died,
then five of his children. Crippled Soren survived.
The self-consuming sickness unto death is despair.

What the age needs is not a genius but a martyr.
Soren fell in love, proposed, then broke the engagement.
No one, he thought, could bear his presence daily.
My sorrow is my castle. His books were read
but ridiculed. Cartoons mocked his deformities.
His private journals fill seven thousand pages.
You could read them all, he claimed, and still not know him.
He who explains this riddle explains my life.

When everyone is Christian, Christianity
does not exist. The crowd is untruth. Remember
we stand alone before God in fear and trembling.
At forty-two he collapsed on his daily walk.
Dying he seemed radiant. His skin had become
almost transparent. He refused communion
from the established church. His grave has no headstone.
Now with God's help I shall at last become myself.

· II ·

PLACE

CALIFORNIA HILLS IN AUGUST

I can imagine someone who found
these fields unbearable, who climbed
the hillside in the heat, cursing the dust,
cracking the brittle weeds underfoot,
wishing a few more trees for shade.

An Easterner especially, who would scorn
the meagerness of summer, the dry
twisted shapes of black elm,
scrub oak, and chaparral, a landscape
August has already drained of green.

One who would hurry over the clinging
thistle, foxtail, golden poppy,
knowing everything was just a weed,
unable to conceive that these trees
and sparse brown bushes were alive.

And hate the bright stillness of the noon
without wind, without motion,
the only other living thing
a hawk, hungry for prey, suspended
in the blinding, sunlit blue.

And yet how gentle it seems to someone
raised in a landscape short of rain—
the skyline of a hill broken by no more
trees than one can count, the grass,
the empty sky, the wish for water.

CRUISING WITH THE BEACH BOYS

So strange to hear that song again tonight
Traveling on business in a rented car
Miles from anywhere I've been before.
And now a tune I haven't heard for years
Probably not since it last left the charts
Back in L.A. in 1969.
I can't believe I know the words by heart
And can't think of a girl to blame them on.

Every lovesick summer has its song,
And this one I pretended to despise,
But if I was alone when it came on,
I turned it up full-blast to sing along—
A primal scream in croaky baritone,
The notes all flat, the lyrics mostly slurred.
No wonder I spent so much time alone
Making the rounds in Dad's old Thunderbird.

Some nights I drove down to the beach to park
And walk along the railings of the pier.
The water down below was cold and dark,
The waves monotonous against the shore.
The darkness and the mist, the midnight sea,
The flickering lights reflected from the city—
A perfect setting for a boy like me,
The Cecil B. DeMille of my self-pity.

I thought by now I'd left those nights behind,
Lost like the girls that I could never get,
Gone with the years, junked with the old T-Bird.
But one old song, a stretch of empty road,
Can open up a door and let them fall
Tumbling like boxes from a dusty shelf,
Tightening my throat for no reason at all,
Bringing on tears shed only for myself.

California night. The Devil's wind,
the Santa Ana, blows in from the east,
raging through the canyon like a drunk
screaming in a bar.
                            The air tastes like
a stubbed-out cigarette. But why complain?
The weather's fine as long as you don't breathe.
Just lean back on the sweat-stained furniture,
lights turned out, windows shut against the storm,
and count your blessings.
                            Another sleepless night,
when every wrinkle in the bedsheet scratches
like a dry razor on a sunburned cheek,
when even ten-year whiskey tastes like sand,
and quiet women in the kitchen run
their fingers on the edges of a knife
and eye their husbands' necks. I wish them luck.

Tonight it seems that if I took the coins
out of my pocket and tossed them in the air
they'd stay a moment glistening like a net
slowly falling through dark water.
                            I remember
the headlights of the cars parked on the beach,
the narrow beams dissolving on the dark
surface of the lake, voices arguing
about the forms, the crackling radio,
the sheeted body lying on the sand,
the trawling net still damp beside it. No,
she wasn't beautiful—but at that age
when youth itself becomes a kind of beauty—
"Taking good care of your clients, Marlowe?"

Relentlessly the wind blows on. Next door
catching a scent, the dogs begin to howl.
Lean, furious, raw-eyed from the storm,
packs of coyotes come down from the hills
where there is nothing left to hunt.

IN CHEEVER COUNTRY

Half an hour north of Grand Central
the country opens up. Through the rattling
grime-streaked windows of the coach, streams appear,
pine trees gather into woods, and the leaf-swept yards
grow large enough to seem picturesque.

Farther off smooth parkways curve along the rivers,
trimmed by well-kept trees, and the County Airport
now boasts seven lines, but to know this country
see it from a train—even this crowded local
jogging home half an hour before dark

smelling of smoke and rain-damp shoes
on an afternoon of dodging sun and showers.
One trip without a book or paper
will show enough to understand
this landscape no ones takes too seriously.

The architecture of each station still preserves
its fantasy beside the sordid tracks—
defiant pergolas, a shuttered summer lodge,
a shadowy pavilion framed by high-arched windows
in this land of northern sun and lingering winter.

The town names stenciled on the platform signs—
Clear Haven, Bullet Park, and Shady Hill—
show that developers at least believe in poetry
if only as a talisman against the commonplace.
There always seems so much to guard against.

The sunset broadens for a moment, and the passengers
standing on the platform turn strangely luminous
in the light streaming from the Palisades across the river.
Some board the train. Others greet their arrivals
shaking hands and embracing in the dusk.

If there is an afterlife, let it be a small town
gentle as this spot at just this instant.
But the car doors close, and the bright crowd,
unaware of its election, disperses to the small
pleasures of the evening. The platform falls behind.

The train gathers speed. Stations are farther apart.
Marble staircases climb the hills where derelict estates
glimmer in the river-brightened dusk.
Some are convents now, some orphanages,
these palaces the Robber Barons gave to God.

And some are merely left to rot where now
broken stone lions guard a roofless colonnade,
a half-collapsed gazebo bursts with tires,
and each detail warns it is not so difficult
to make a fortune as to pass it on.

But splendor in ruins is splendor still,
even glimpsed from a passing train,
and it is wonderful to imagine standing
in the balustraded gardens above the river
where barges still ply their distant commerce.

Somewhere upstate huge factories melt ore,
mills weave fabric on enormous looms,
and sweeping combines glean the cash-green fields.
Fortunes are made. Careers advance like armies.
But here so little happens that is obvious.

Here in the odd light of a rainy afternoon
a ledger is balanced and put away,
a houseguest knots his tie beside a bed,
and a hermit thrush sings in the unsold lot
next to the tracks the train comes hurtling down.

Finally it's dark outside. Through the freight houses
and oil tanks the train begins to slow
approaching the station where rows of travel posters
and empty benches wait along the platform.
Outside a few cars idle in a sudden shower.

And this at last is home, this ordinary town
where the lights on the hill gleaming in the rain
are the lights that children bathe by, and it is time
to go home now—to drinks, to love, to supper,
to the modest places which contain our lives.

THE GARDEN ON THE CAMPAGNA

Noon—and the shadows of the trees
have fallen from the branches. The frail
blue butterflies still flutter hungrily
among the weeds, and a few pale flowers
climb up the yellow hill and fade away.
The scarred brown lizards lie immobile
in the dust. A line of ants
picks clean the carcass of a frog.

Only the smallest things survive
in this exhausted land the gods
so long ago abandoned. Time
and rain have washed the hero's face
from off the statue. The sundial
stands perpetually in shade.

The bankrupt palace still remains
beyond the wall that summer builds,
doors bolted shut, the roof caved in,
the ancient family without heirs,
and one half-blind old man who sits
each day beside the empty pond
mumbling to himself in dialect.
The village boys throw stones at him,
but he will never leave, and there
is no one left who knows if he
was once the servant or the sire.

MOST JOURNEYS COME TO THIS

an Italy of the mind
—WALLACE STEVENS

I.

Leave the museums, the comfortable rooms,
the safe distractions of the masterpiece.
The broken goddesses have lost their voice,
the martyr's folded hands no longer bless.
Footsteps echo through the palaces
where no one lives. Consider what you've come for.

Leave the museums. Find the dark churches
in back towns that history has forgotten,
the unimportant places the powerful ignore
where commerce knows no profit will be made.
Sad hamlets at the end of silted waterways,
dry mountain villages where time
is the thin shadow of an ancient tower
that moves across the sundazed pavement of the square
and disappears each evening without trace.

Make the slow climb up the winding alleys.
Walk between houses shuttered close for midday
and overhear the sound of other lives,
the conversations in the language you
will never learn. Make the long ascent
up to the gray stone chapel on the hillside
when summer is a furnace open to the world,
and pause there breathless in the blinding sun
only one moment, then enter.

                                        For this
is how it must be seen to understand:
by walking from the sunlight into darkness,
by groping down the aisle
as your wet skin cools and your eyes adjust,
by finding what you've come for thoughtlessly,
shoved off into a corner, almost lost
among the spectacle of gold and purple.

Here in the half-light, covered by the years
it will exist. And wait,
wait like a mirror in an empty room
whose resolutions are invisible
to anyone but you. Wait like the stone
face of a statue waits, forever frozen
or poised in the moment before action.

                        II.

But if the vision fails, and the damp air
stinks of summer must and disrepair,
if the worn steps rising to the altar
lead nowhere but to stone, this, too, could be
the revelation—but of a destiny
fixed as the graceless frescoes on the wall—
the grim and superannuated gods
who rule this shadow-land of marble tombs,
bathed in its green suboceanic light.
Not a vision to pursue, and yet
these insufficiencies make up the world.
Strange how most journeys come to this: the sun
bright on the unfamiliar hills, new vistas
dazzling the eye, the stubborn heart unchanged.

WAITING IN THE AIRPORT

On the same journey each of them
Is going somewhere else. A goose-necked
Woman in a flowered dress
Stares gravely at two businessmen.
They turn away but carry on
Their argument on real estate.

Lost in a mist of aftershave,
A salesman in a brown toupée
Is scribbling on his *Racing Form*
While a fat man stares down at his hands
As if there should be something there.

The soldiers stand in line for sex—
With wives or girlfriends, whoever
They hope is waiting for them at
The other end. The wrapped perfume,
The bright, stuffed animals they clutch
Tremble under so much heat.

Lives have been pulled cross-continent.
So much will soon be going on
But somewhere else—divorces, birthdays,
Deaths and million-dollar deals.

But nothing ever happens here,
This terminal that narrows to
A single unattended gate,
One entrance to so many worlds.

MEN AFTER WORK

Done with work, they are sitting by themselves
in coffeeshops or diners, taking up the booths,
filling every other seat along the counter,
waiting for the menu, for the water,
for the girl to come and take their order,
always on the edge of words, almost without appetite,
knowing there is nothing on the menu that they want,
waiting patiently to ask for one
more refill of their coffee, surprised
that even its bitterness will not wake them up.
Still they savor it, holding each sip
lukewarm in their mouths, this last taste of evening.

ROUGH COUNTRY

Give me a landscape made of obstacles,
of steep hills and jutting glacial rock,
where the low-running streams are quick to flood
the grassy fields and bottomlands.
                                                    A place
no engineers can master—where the roads
must twist like tendrils up the mountainside
on narrow cliffs where boulders block the way.

Where tall black trunks of lightning-scalded pine
push through the tangled woods to make a roost
for hawks and swarming crows.
                                                    And sharp inclines
where twisting through the thorn-thick underbrush,
scratched and exhausted, one turns suddenly

to find an unexpected waterfall,
not half a mile from the nearest road,
a spot so hard to reach that no one comes—

a hiding place, a shrine for dragonflies
and nesting jays, a sign that there is still
one piece of property that won't be owned.

BECOMING A REDWOOD

Stand in a field long enough, and the sounds
start up again. The crickets, the invisible
toad who claims that change is possible,

And all the other life too small to name.
First one, then another, until innumerable
they merge into the single voice of a summer hill.

Yes, it's hard to stand still, hour after hour,
fixed as a fencepost, hearing the steers
snort in the dark pasture, smelling the manure.

And paralyzed by the mystery of how a stone
can bear to be a stone, the pain
the grass endures breaking through the earth's crust.

Unimaginable the redwoods on the far hill,
rooted for centuries, the living wood grown tall
and thickened with a hundred thousand days of light.

The old windmill creaks in perfect time
to the wind shaking the miles of pasture grass,
and the last farmhouse light goes off.

Something moves nearby. Coyotes hunt
these hills and packs of feral dogs.
But standing here at night accepts all that.

You are your own pale shadow in the quarter moon,
moving more slowly than the crippled stars,
part of the moonlight as the moonlight falls,

Part of the grass that answers the wind,
part of the midnight's watchfulness that knows
there is no silence but when danger comes.

A CALIFORNIA REQUIEM

I walked among the equidistant graves
New planted in the irrigated lawn.
The square, trim headstones quietly declared
The impotence of grief against the sun.

There were no outward signs of human loss.
No granite angel wept beside the lane.
No bending willow broke the once-rough ground
Now graded to a geometric plane.

My blessed California, you are so wise.
You render death abstract, efficient, clean.
Your afterlife is only real estate,
And in his kingdom Death must stay unseen.

I would have left then. I had made my one
Obligatory visit to the dead.
But as I turned to go, I heard the voices,
Faint but insistent. This is what they said.

"Stay a moment longer, quiet stranger.
Your footsteps woke us from our lidded cells.
Now hear us whisper in the scorching wind,
Our single voice drawn from a thousand hells.

"We lived in places that we never knew.
We could not name the birds perched on our sill,
Or see the trees we cut down for our view.
What we possessed we always chose to kill.

"We claimed the earth but did not hear her claim,
And when we died, they laid us on her breast,
But she refuses us—until we earn
Forgiveness from the lives we dispossessed.

"We are so tiny now—light as the spores
That rotting clover sheds into the air,
Dry as old pods burnt open by the sun,
Barren as seeds unrooted anywhere.

"Forget your stylish verses, little poet—
So sadly beautiful, precise, and tame.
We are your people, though you would deny it.
Admit the justice of our primal claim.

"Become the voice of our forgotten places.
Teach us the names of what we have destroyed.
We are like shadows the bright noon erases,
Weightlessly shrinking, bleached into the void.

"We offer you the landscape of your birth—
Exquisite and despoiled. We all share blame.
We cannot ask forgiveness of the earth
For killing what we cannot even name."

THE END OF THE WORLD

"We're going," they said, "to the end of the world."
So they stopped the car where the river curled,
And we scrambled down beneath the bridge
On the gravel track of a narrow ridge.

We tramped for miles on a wooded walk
Where dog-hobble grew on its twisted stalk.
Then we stopped to rest on the pine-needle floor
While two ospreys watched from an oak by the shore.

We came to a bend, where the river grew wide
And green mountains rose on the opposite side.
My guides moved back. I stood alone,
As the current streaked over smooth flat stone.

Shelf by stone shelf the river fell.
The white water goosetailed with eddying swell.
Faster and louder the current dropped
Till it reached a cliff, and the trail stopped.

I stood at the edge where the mist ascended,
My journey done where the world ended.
I looked downstream. There was nothing but sky,
The sound of the water, and the water's reply.

SHOPPING

I enter the temple of my people but do not pray.
I pass the altars of the gods but do not kneel
Or offer sacrifices proper to the season.

Strolling the hushed aisles of the department store,
I see visions shining under glass,
Divinities of leather, gold, and porcelain,
Shrines of cut crystal, stainless steel, and silicon.

But I wander the arcades of abundance,
Empty of desire, no credit to my people,
Envying the acolytes their passionate faith.
Blessed are the acquisitive,
For theirs is the kingdom of commerce.

Redeem me, gods of the mall and marketplace.
Mercury, protector of cell phones and fax machines,
Venus, patroness of bath and bedroom chains,
Tantalus, guardian of the food court.

Beguile me with the aromas of coffee, musk, and cinnamon.
Surround me with delicately colored soaps and moisturizing creams.
Comfort me with posters of children with perfect smiles
And pouting teenage models clad in lingerie.
I am not made of stone.

Show me satins, linen, crêpe de chine, and silk,
Heaped like cumuli in the morning sky,
As if all caravans and argosies ended in this parking lot
To fill these stockrooms and loading docks.

Sing me the hymns of no cash down and the installment plan,
Of custom fit, remote control, and priced to move.
Whisper the blessing of Egyptian cotton, polyester, and cashmere.
Tell me in what department my desire shall be found.

Because I would buy happiness if I could find it,
Spend all that I possessed or could borrow.
But what can I bring you from these sad emporia?
Where in this splendid clutter
Shall I discover the one true thing?

Nothing to carry, I should stroll easily
Among the crowded countertops and eager cashiers,
Bypassing the sullen lines and footsore customers,
Spending only my time, discounting all I see.

Instead I look for you among the pressing crowds,
But they know nothing of you, turning away,
Carrying their brightly packaged burdens.
There is no angel among the vending stalls and signage.

Where are you, my fugitive? Without you
There is nothing but the getting and the spending
Of things that have a price.
Why else have I stalked the leased arcades
Searching the kiosks and the cash machines?

Where are you, my errant soul and innermost companion?
Are you outside amid the potted palm trees,
Bumming a cigarette or joking with the guards,
Or are you wandering the parking lot
Lost among the rows of Subarus and Audis?

Or is that you I catch a sudden glimpse of
Smiling behind the greasy window of the bus
As it disappears into the evening rush?

SEA PEBBLES: AN ELEGY

My love, how time makes hardness shine.
They come in every color, pure or mixed,
gray-green of basalt, blood-soaked jasper, quartz,
granite and feldspar, even bits of glass,
smoothed by the patient jeweller of the tides.

Volcano-born, earthquake-quarried,
shaven by glaciers, wind-carved, heat-cracked,
stratified, speckled, bright in the wet surf—
no two alike, all torn from the dry land
tossed up in millions on this empty shore.

How small death seems among the rocks. It drifts
light as a splintered bone the tide uncovers.
It glints among the shattered oyster shells,
gutted by gulls, bleached by salt and sun—
the broken crockery of living things.

Cormorants glide across the quiet bay.
A falcon watches from the ridge, indifferent
to the burdens I have carried here.
No point in walking farther, so I sit,
hollow as driftwood, dead as any stone.

VULTURES MATING

On the branch of a large dead tree
a vulture sits, stinking of carrion.
She is ripe with the perfume of her fertility.
Half a dozen males circle above her,
slowly gliding on the thermals.

One by one, the huge birds settle
stiffly beside her on the limb,
stretching their wings, inflating their chests,
holding their red scabrous heads erect.
Their nostrils dilate with desire.

The ritual goes on for hours.
These bald scavengers pay court politely—
like overdressed princes in an old romance—
circling, stretching, yearning,
waiting for her to choose.

The stink and splendor of fertility
arouses the world. The rotting log
flowers with green moss. The fallen chestnut
splits and drives its root into the soil.
The golden air pours down its pollen.

Desire brings all things back to earth,
charging them to circle, stretch, and preen—
the buzzard or the princess, the scorpion, the rose—
each damp and fecund bud yearning to burst,
to burn, to blossom, to begin.

PROGRESS REPORT

It's time to admit I'm irresponsible.
I lack ambition. I get nothing done.

I spend the morning walking up the fire road.
I know every tree along the ridge.

Reaching the end, I turn around. There's no point
to my pilgrimage except the coming and the going.

Then I sit and listen to the woodpecker
tapping away. He works too hard.

Tonight I will go out to watch the moon rise.
If only I could move that slowly.

I have no plans. No one visits me.
No need to change my clothes.

What a blessing just to sit still—
a luxury only the lazy can afford.

Let the dusk settle on my desk.
No one needs to hear from me today.

· III ·

REMEMBRANCE

To the memory of my first son

Michael Jasper Gioia

Briefest of joys, our life together.

PRAYER

Echo of the clocktower, footstep
in the alleyway, sweep
of the wind sifting the leaves.

Jeweller of the spiderweb, connoisseur
of autumn's opulence, blade of lightning
harvesting the sky.

Keeper of the small gate, choreographer
of entrances and exits, midnight
whisper traveling the wires.

Seducer, healer, deity or thief,
I will see you soon enough—
in the shadow of the rainfall,

in the brief violet darkening a sunset—
but until then I pray watch over him
as a mountain guards its covert ore

and the harsh falcon its flightless young.

NIGHT WATCH

For my uncle, Theodore Ortiz, U.S.M.M.

I think of you standing on the sloping deck
as the freighter pulls away from the coast of China,
the last lights of Asia disappearing in the fog,
and the engine's drone dissolving in the old
monotony of waves slapping up against the hull.

Leaning on the rails, looking eastward to America
across the empty weeks of ocean,
how carefully you must have planned your life,
so much of it already wasted on the sea,
the vast country of your homelessness.

Macao. Vladivostok. Singapore.
Dante read by shiplamp on the bridge.
The names of fellow sailors lost in war.
These memories will die with you,
but tonight they rise up burning in your mind

interweaving like gulls crying in the wake,
like currents on a chart, like gulfweed
swirling in a star-soaked sea, and interchangeable
as all the words for night—*la notte, noche, Nacht, nuit,*
each sound half-foreign, half-familiar, like America.

For now you know that mainland best from dreams.
Your dead mother turning toward you slowly,
always on the edge of words, yet always
silent as the suffering Madonna of a shrine.
Or your father pounding his fist against the wall.

There are so many ways to waste a life.
Why choose between these icons of unhappiness,
when there is the undisguised illusion of the sea,
the comfort of old books and solitude to fill
the long night watch, the endless argument of waves?

Breathe in that dark and tangible air, for in a few weeks
you will be dead, burned beyond recognition,
left as a headstone in the unfamiliar earth
with no one to ask, neither wife nor children,
why your thin ashes have been buried here

and not scattered on the shifting gray Pacific.

VETERANS' CEMETERY

The ceremonies of the day have ceased,
Abandoned to the ragged crow's parade.
The flags unravel in the caterpillar's feast.
The wreaths collapse onto the stones they shade.

How quietly doves gather by the gate
Like souls who have no heaven and no hell.
The patient grass reclaims its lost estate
Where one stone angel stands as sentinel.

The voices whispering in the burning leaves,
Faint and inhuman, what can they desire
When every season feeds upon the past,
And summer's green ignites the autumn's fire?

The afternoon's a single thread of light
Sewn through the tatters of a leafless willow,
As one by one the branches fade from sight,
And time curls up like paper turning yellow.

THE SONG

How shall I hold my soul that it
does not touch yours? How shall I lift
it over you to other things?
If it would only sink below
into the dark like some lost thing
or slumber in some quiet place
which did not echo your soft heart's beat.
But all that ever touched us—you and me—
touched us together
                    like a bow
that from two strings could draw one voice.
On what instrument were we strung?
And to what player did we sing
our interrupted song?

(After the German of Rainer Maria Rilke)

THE GODS OF WINTER

Storm on storm, snow on drifting snowfall,
shifting its shape, flurrying in moonlight,
bright and ubiquitous,
profligate March squanders its wealth.
The world is annihilated and remade
with only us as witnesses.

Briefest of joys, our life together,
this brittle flower twisting toward the light
even as it dies, no more permanent
for being perfect. Time will melt away
triumphant winter, and even your touch
prove the unpossessable jewel of ice.

And vanish like this unseasonable storm
drifting there beyond the windows where even
the cluttered rooftops now lie soft and luminous
like a storybook view of paradise.
Why not believe these suave messengers
of starlight? Morning will make

their brightness blinding, and the noon insist
that only legend saves the beautiful. But if
the light confides how one still winter must
arrive without us, then our eternity
is only this white storm, the whisper
of your breath, the deities of this quiet night.

PLANTING A SEQUOIA

All afternoon my brothers and I have worked in the orchard,
Digging this hole, laying you into it, carefully packing the soil.
Rain blackened the horizon, but cold winds kept it over the Pacific,
And the sky above us stayed the dull gray
Of an old year coming to an end.

In Sicily a father plants a tree to celebrate his first son's birth—
An olive or a fig tree—a sign that the earth has one more life to bear.
I would have done the same, proudly laying new stock into my
    father's orchard,
A green sapling rising among the twisted apple boughs,
A promise of new fruit in other autumns.

But today we kneel in the cold planting you, our native giant,
Defying the practical custom of our fathers,
Wrapping in your roots a lock of hair, a piece of an infant's birth cord,
All that remains above earth of a first-born son,
A few stray atoms brought back to the elements.

We will give you what we can—our labor and our soil,
Water drawn from the earth when the skies fail,
Nights scented with the ocean fog, days softened by the circuit of bees.
We plant you in the corner of the grove, bathed in western light,
A slender shoot against the sunset.

And when our family is no more, all of his unborn brothers dead,
Every niece and nephew scattered, the house torn down,
His mother's beauty ashes in the air,
I want you to stand among strangers, all young and ephemeral to you,
Silently keeping the secret of your birth.

METAMORPHOSIS

There were a few, the old ones promised us,
Who could escape. A few who once, when trapped
At the extremes of violence, reached out
Beyond the rapist's hand or sudden blade.

Their fingers branched and blossomed. Or they leapt
Unthinking from the heavy earth to fly
With voices—ever softer—that became
The admonitions of the nightingale.
They proved, like cornered Daphne twisting free,
There were a few whom even the great gods
Could not destroy.

        And you, my gentle ghost,
Did you break free before the cold hand clutched?
Did you escape into the lucid air
Or burrow secretly among the dark
Expectant roots, to rise again with them
As the unknown companion of our spring?

I'll never know, my changeling, where you've gone,
And so I'll praise you—flower, bird, and tree—
My nightingale awake among the thorns,
My laurel tree that marks a god's defeat,
My blossom bending on the water's edge,
Forever lost within your inward gaze.

PENTECOST

After the death of our son

Neither the sorrows of afternoon, waiting in the silent house,
Nor the night no sleep relieves, when memory
Repeats its prosecution.

Nor the morning's ache for dream's illusion, nor any prayers
Improvised to an unknowable god
Can extinguish the flame.

We are not as we were. Death has been our pentecost,
And our innocence consumed by these implacable
Tongues of fire.

Comfort me with stones. Quench my thirst with sand.
I offer you this scarred and guilty hand
Until others mix our ashes.

THE LITANY

This is a litany of lost things,
a canon of possessions dispossessed,
a photograph, an old address, a key.
It is a list of words to memorize
or to forget—of *amo, amas, amat,*
the conjugations of a dead tongue
in which the final sentence has been spoken.

This is the liturgy of rain,
falling on mountain, field, and ocean—
indifferent, anonymous, complete—
of water infinitesimally slow,
sifting through rock, pooling in darkness,
gathering in springs, then rising without our agency,
only to dissolve in mist or cloud or dew.

This is a prayer to unbelief,
to candles guttering and darkness undivided,
to incense drifting into emptiness.
It is the smile of a stone Madonna
and the silent fury of the consecrated wine,
a benediction on the death of a young god,
brave and beautiful, rotting on a tree.

This is a litany to earth and ashes,
to the dust of roads and vacant rooms,
to the fine silt circling in a shaft of sun,
settling indifferently on books and beds.
This is a prayer to praise what we become,
"Dust thou art, to dust thou shalt return."
Savor its taste—the bitterness of earth and ashes.

This is a prayer, inchoate and unfinished,
for you, my love, my loss, my lesion,
a rosary of words to count out time's
illusions, all the minutes, hours, days
the calendar compounds as if the past
existed somewhere—like an inheritance
still waiting to be claimed.

Until at last it is our litany, *mon vieux,*
my reader, my voyeur, as if the mist
steaming from the gorge, this pure paradox,
the shattered river rising as it falls—
splintering the light, swirling it skyward,
neither transparent nor opaque but luminous,
even as it vanishes—were not our life.

UNSAID

So much of what we live goes on inside—
The diaries of grief, the tongue-tied aches
Of unacknowledged love are no less real
For having passed unsaid. What we conceal
Is always more than what we dare confide.
Think of the letters that we write our dead.

FINDING A BOX OF FAMILY LETTERS

The dead say little in their letters
they haven't said before.
We find no secrets, and yet
how different every sentence sounds
heard across the years.

My father breaks my heart
simply by being so young and handsome.
He's half my age, with jet-black hair.
Look at him in his navy uniform
grinning beside his dive-bomber.

Come back, Dad! I want to shout.
He says he misses all of us
(though I haven't yet been born).
He writes from places I never knew he saw,
and everyone he mentions now is dead.

There is a large, long photograph
curled like a diploma—a banquet sixty years ago.
My parents sit uncomfortably
among tables of dark-suited strangers.
The mildewed paper reeks of regret.

I wonder what song the band was playing,
just out of frame, as the photographer
arranged your smiles. A waltz? A foxtrot?
Get out there on the floor and dance!
You don't have forever.

What does it cost to send a postcard
to the underworld? I'll buy
a penny stamp from World War II
and mail it downtown at the old post office
just as the courthouse clock strikes twelve.

Surely the ghost of some postal worker
still makes his nightly rounds, his routine
too tedious for him to notice when it ended.
He works so slowly he moves back in time
carrying our dead letters to their lost addresses.

It's silly to get sentimental.
The dead have moved on. So should we.
But isn't it equally simple-minded to miss
the special expertise of the departed
in clarifying our long-term plans?

They never let us forget that the line
between them and us is only temporary.
Get out there and dance! the letters shout
adding, *Love always. Can't wait to get home!*
And soon we will be. *See you there.*

SPECIAL TREATMENTS WARD

I.

So this is where the children come to die,
hidden on the hospital's highest floor.
They wear their bandages like uniforms
and pull their IV rigs along the hall
with slow and careful steps. Or bald and pale,
they lie in bright pajamas on their beds,
watching another world on a screen.

The mothers spend their nights inside the ward,
sleeping on chairs that fold out into beds,
too small to lie in comfort. Soon they slip
beside their children, as if they might mesh
those small bruised bodies back into their flesh.
Instinctively they feel that love so strong
protects a child. Each morning proves them wrong.

No one chooses to be here. We play the parts
that we are given—horrible as they are.
We try to play them well, whatever that means.
We need to talk, though talking breaks our hearts.
The doctors come and go like oracles,
their manner cool, omniscient, and oblique.
There is a word that no one ever speaks.

II.

I put this poem aside twelve years ago
because I could not bear remembering
the faces it evoked, and every line
seemed—still seems—so inadequate and grim.

What right had I whose son had walked away
to speak for those who died? And I'll admit
I wanted to forget. I'd lost one child
and couldn't bear to watch another die.

Not just the silent boy who shared our room,
but even the bird-thin figures dimly glimpsed
shuffling deliberately, disjointedly
like ancient soldiers after a parade.

Whatever strength the task required I lacked.
No well-stitched words could suture shut these wounds.
And so I stopped . . .
But there are poems we do not choose to write.

III.

The children visit me, not just in dream,
appearing suddenly, silently—
insistent, unprovoked, unwelcome.

They've taken off their milky bandages
to show the raw, red lesions they still bear.
Risen they are healed but not made whole.

A few I recognize, untouched by years.
I cannot name them—their faces pale and gray
like ashes fallen from a distant fire.

What use am I to them, almost a stranger?
I cannot wake them from their satin beds.
Why do they seek me? They never speak.

And vagrant sorrow cannot bless the dead.

MAJORITY

Now you'd be three,
I said to myself,
seeing a child born
the same summer as you.

Now you'd be six,
or seven, or ten.
I watched you grow
in foreign bodies.

Leaping into a pool, all laughter,
or frowning over a keyboard,
but mostly just standing,
taller each time.

How splendid your most
mundane action seemed
in these joyful proxies.
I often held back tears.

Now you are twenty-one.
Finally, it makes sense
that you have moved away
into your own afterlife.

MY HANDSOME COUSIN

I saw you in a dream last night—
Quiet and pale, but still my handsome cousin.
Your hair was thick and glossy black.

Your breath was earthy whispering in my ear.
"I'm not dead," you told me. "I've been away.
I've come to show you the house I've bought."

We walked together through the empty rooms.
Each one was smaller than the room before.
"And this," you smiled, "will be the nursery."

I thought of your children, now full-grown,
Who know you from old photographs,
And of your widow, beautiful but gray.

I wanted to ask where you had gone,
But you spoke first, "It's time to go next door.
Let's see the house that will be yours."

· IV ·

IMAGINATION

ELEGY FOR VLADIMIR DE PACHMANN

(Odessa, 1848–Rome, 1933)

"How absurd," cried the pianist de Pachmann
    to reporters from the *Minneapolis Dispatch,*
"that my talents or the talents of a Liszt
    were confined to so small a planet
as the earth. How much more could we have done
    given the dimensions of a fixed star?"
He began a prelude quietly, then stopped.
    "Once Chopin could play this well. Now only me."

When he brought his socks into the concert hall
    and dedicated that night's music to them,
or relearned his repertoire at sixty-nine
    using only the fourth and fifth fingers
of one hand, the critics thought his madness
    was theatrical, but the less learned
members of his audience, to whom he talked
    while playing, knew the truth.

Porters and impresarios told of coming on him,
    alone in a hotel suite, his back
curved like a monkey's, dancing and screeching
    in front of a dressing mirror,
or giving concerts for the velvet furniture
    in his room, knocking it together afterwards
for applause. "Dear friends," he whispered to it,
    "such love deserves an encore."

Now relegated to three short paragraphs
in *Grove's Dictionary of Music*
and one out-of-stock recording of Chopin,
he reappears only by schedule
in a few selections broadcast on his birthday,
music produced by rolls on a mechanical piano
where no fingers touch the keys as each piece
goes to its predictable finale.

LIVES OF THE GREAT COMPOSERS

Herr Bruckner often wandered into church
to join the mourners at a funeral.
The relatives of Berlioz were horrified.
"Such harmony," quoth Shakespeare, "is in
immortal souls. . . . We cannot hear it." But
the radio is playing, and outside
rain splashes to the pavement. Now and then
the broadcast fails. On nights like these Schumann
would watch the lightning streak his windowpanes.

Outside the rain is falling on the pavement.
A scrap of paper tumbles down the street.
On rainy evenings Schumann jotted down
his melodies on windowpanes. "Such harmony!
We cannot hear it." The radio goes off and on.
At the rehearsal Gustav Holst exclaimed,
"I'm sick of music, especially my own!"
The relatives of Berlioz were horrified.
Haydn's wife used music to line pastry pans.

On rainy nights the ghost of Mendelssohn
brought melodies for Schumann to compose.
"Such harmony is in immortal souls. . . .
We cannot hear it." One could suppose
Herr Bruckner would have smiled. At Tegernsee
the peasants stood to hear young Paganini play,
but here there's lightning, and the thunder rolls.
The radio goes off and on. The rain
falls to the pavement like applause.

A scrap of paper tumbles down the street.
On rainy evenings Schumann would look out
and scribble on the windows of his cell.
"Such harmony." Cars splash out in the rain.
The relatives of Berlioz were horrified
to see the horses break from the cortege
and gallop with his casket to the grave.
Liszt wept to hear old Paganini play.
Haydn's wife used music to line pastry pans.

GOD ONLY KNOWS

Here is the church,
Here is the steeple,
Open it up,
And see all the people.

God only knows

if Bach's greatest work
was just an improvised
accompaniment
between two verses of a hymn,
one that stopped the burghers
squirming in their pews
and made them not only
listen to the organ in the loft
but actually hear the roof
unbend itself
and leave the church wide
open to a terrifying sky
which he had filled with angels
holding ledgers
for a roll call of the damned,
whom they would have named,
had not the congregation
started up the final chorus
and sung

to save their souls.

A CURSE ON GEOGRAPHERS

We want an earth to walk upon,
Not reasons to remain at home.
Shall we make journeys only to see
The same stars circling in the night?
Eat the same fish in foreign harbors?
Breathe the same air? Sail across
These oceans only to discover
Our own island's other shore?

Let the oceans spill their green from off
The edges of the earth, and let
The curving plain unbend itself
Behind the mountains. Put wind back
Into the cheeks of demons. Voice,
Pronounce your reasonable desire
And sing the round earth flat again!

A SHORT HISTORY OF TOBACCO

Profitable, poisonous, and purely American—
it was Columbus who discovered it
on reaching China, noticing the leaves
in a canoe. He sent his men ashore
to find the Great Khan's palace. They returned
to tell of squatting natives who drank smoke.

Rolfe smuggled seeds to cold, bankrupt Virginia.
When he returned years later, all the streets
were planted with the crop, the marketplace
and churchyards overgrown. Grim ministers
preached harvest from the pulpit and stood out
among the fields at night to guard their tithes.

More valuable than silver, worth ten times
the price of peppercorn. In Africa
six rolls could buy a man. The ships would reach
Virginia stocked with slaves or English wives
while every year the farms moved farther west
abandoning their dry, exhausted fields.

Tenacious, fertile, rank as any weed,
Linnaeus counted forty thousand seeds
inside one pod. *Miraculus,* he wrote,
the cure for toothache, shingles, running sores
or, pushed by bellows through a patient's lung,
the panacea of the alchemists.

Fragrant, prophylactic, and medicinal,
Pepys chewed it during the Great Plague.
It cost a fortune, but it saved his life.
Later he spent an afternoon to watch
a surgeon fill a cat with just one drop
of the quintessence of Virginia leaf.

. . . But when a bear was killed, tobacco smoke
was blown into his throat to soothe the spirit.
The elders smoked and chanted in a trance.
The Mayans blew the smoke to the four corners
of the world. It was a gift from God—
profitable, poisonous, and purely American.

This is the hall of broken limbs
Where splintered marble athletes lie
Beside the arms of cherubim.
Nothing is ever thrown away.

These butterflies are set in rows.
So small and gray inside their case
They look alike now. I suppose
Death makes most creatures commonplace.

These portraits here of the unknown
Are hung three high, frame piled on frame.
Each potent soul who craved renown,
Immortalized without a name.

Here are the shelves of unread books,
Millions of pages turning brown.
Visitors wander through the stacks,
But no one ever takes one down.

I wish I were a better guide.
There's so much more that you should see—
Rows of bottles with nothing inside,
Displays of locks which have no key.

You'd like to go? I wish you could.
This room has such a peaceful view.
Look at that case of antique wood
Without a label. It's for you.

MY CONFESSIONAL SESTINA

Let me confess. I'm sick of these sestinas
written by youngsters in poetry workshops
for the delectation of their fellow students,
and then published in little magazines
that no one reads, not even the contributors
who at least in this omission show some taste.

Is this merely a matter of personal taste?
I don't think so. Most sestinas
are such dull affairs. Just ask the contributors
the last time they finished one outside of a workshop,
even the poignant one on herpes in that new little magazine
edited by their most brilliant fellow student.

Let's be honest. It has become a form for students,
an exercise to build technique rather than taste
and the official entry blank into the little magazines—
because despite its reputation, a passable sestina
isn't very hard to write, even for kids in workshops
who care less about being poets than contributors.

Granted nowadays everyone is a contributor.
My barber is currently a student
in a rigorous correspondence school workshop.
At lesson six he can already taste
success having just placed his own sestina
in a national tonsorial magazine.

Who really cares about most little magazines?
Eventually not even their own contributors
who having published a few preliminary sestinas
send their work East to prove they're no longer students.
They need to be recognized as the new arbiters of taste
so they can teach their own graduate workshops.

Where will it end? This grim cycle of workshops
churning out poems for little magazines
no one honestly finds to their taste?
This ever-lengthening column of contributors
scavenging the land for more students,
teaching them to write their boot-camp sestinas?

Perhaps there is an afterlife where all contributors
have two workshops, a tasteful little magazine, and sexy students
who worshipfully memorize their every sestina.

THE SILENCE OF THE POETS

is something to be grateful for.
Once there were so many books, so many poets.
All the masterpieces one could never read,
indistinguishable even then
among the endless shelves of the unreadable.

Some claim the best stopped writing first.
For the others, no one noted when or why.
A few observers voiced their mild regret
about another picturesque, unprofitable craft
that progress had irrevocably doomed.

And what was lost? No one now can judge.
But we still have music, art, and film,
diversions enough for a busy people.
And even poetry for those who want it.
The old books, those the young have not defaced,
are still kept somewhere,
stacked in their dusty rows.

And a few old men may visit from time to time
to run their hands across the spines
and reminisce,
but no one ever comes to read
or would know how.

MONEY

Money is a kind of poetry.
—WALLACE STEVENS

Money, the long green,
cash, stash, rhino, jack
or just plain dough.

Chock it up, fork it over,
shell it out. Watch it
burn holes through pockets.

To be made of it! To have it
to burn! Greenbacks, double eagles,
megabucks and Ginnie Maes.

It greases the palm, feathers a nest,
holds heads above water,
makes both ends meet.

Money breeds money.
Gathering interest, compounding daily.
Always in circulation.

Money. You don't know where it's been,
but you put it where your mouth is.
And it talks.

THE NEXT POEM

How much better it seems now
than when it is finally done—
the unforgettable first line,
the cunning way the stanzas run.

The rhymes soft-spoken and suggestive
are barely audible at first,
an appetite not yet acknowledged
like the inkling of a thirst.

While gradually the form appears
as each line is coaxed aloud—
the architecture of a room
seen from the middle of a crowd.

The music that of common speech
but slanted so that each detail
sounds unexpected as a sharp
inserted in a simple scale.

No jumble box of imagery
dumped glumly in the reader's lap
or elegantly packaged junk
the unsuspecting must unwrap.

But words that could direct a friend
precisely to an unknown place,
those few unshakeable details
that no confusion can erase.

And the real subject left unspoken
but unmistakable to those
who don't expect a jungle parrot
in the black and white of prose.

How much better it seems now
than when it is finally written.
How hungrily one waits to feel
the bright lure seized, the old hook bitten.

ELEGY WITH SURREALIST PROVERBS
AS REFRAIN

"Poetry must lead somewhere," declared Breton.
He carried a rose inside his coat each day
to give a beautiful stranger—"Better to die of love
than love without regret." And those who loved him
soon learned regret. "The simplest surreal act
is running through the street with a revolver
firing at random." Old and famous, he seemed *démodé*.
There is always a skeleton on the buffet.

Wounded Apollinaire wore a small steel plate
inserted in his skull. "I so loved art," he smiled,
"I joined the artillery." His friends were asked to wait
while his widow laid a crucifix across his chest.
Picasso hated death. The funeral left him so distressed
he painted a self-portrait. "It's always other people,"
remarked Duchamp, "who do the dying."
I came. I sat down. I went away.

Dali dreamed of Hitler as a white-skinned girl—
impossibly pale, luminous and lifeless as the moon.
Wealthy Roussel taught his poodle to smoke a pipe.
"When I write, I am surrounded by radiance.
My glory is like a great bomb waiting to explode."
When his valet refused to slash his wrists,
the bankrupt writer took an overdose of pills.
There is always a skeleton on the buffet.

Breton considered suicide the truest art,
though life seemed hardly worth the trouble to discard.
The German colonels strolled the Île de la Cité—
some to the Louvre, some to the Place Pigalle.
"The loneliness of poets has been erased," cried Éluard,
in praise of Stalin. "Burn all the books," said dying Hugo Ball.
There is always a skeleton on the buffet.
I came. I sat down. I went away.

AUTUMN INAUGURAL

I.

There will always be those who reject ceremony,
Who claim that resolution requires no fanfare,
Those who demand the spirit stay fixed
Like a desert saint, fed only on faith,
To worship in no temple but the weather.

There will always be the austere ones
Who mount denial's shaky ladder
To drape the statues or whitewash the frescoed wall,
As if the still star of painted plaster
Praised creation less than the evening's original.

And they are right. Symbols betray us.
They are always more or less than what
Is really meant. But shall there be no
Processions by torchlight because we are weak?
What native speech do we share but imperfection?

II.

Praise to the rituals that celebrate change,
Old robes worn for new beginnings,
Solemn protocol where the mutable soul,
Surrounded by ancient experience, grows
Young in the imagination's white dress.

Because it is not the rituals we honor
But our trust in what they signify, these rites
That honor us as witnesses—whether to watch
Lovers swear loyalty in a careless world
Or a newborn washed with water and oil.

So praise to innocence—impulsive and evergreen—
And let the old be touched by youth's
Wayward astonishment at learning something new,
And dream of a future so fitting and so just
That our desire will bring it into being.

THE SEVEN DEADLY SINS

Forget about the other six, says Pride.
They're only using you.
Admittedly, Lust is a looker,
but you can do better.

And why do they keep bringing us
to this cheesy dive?
The food's so bad that even Gluttony
can't finish his meal.

Notice how Avarice
keeps refilling his glass
whenever he thinks we're not looking,
while Envy eyes your plate.

Hell, we're not even done, and Anger
is already arguing about the bill.
I'm the only one who
ever leaves a decent tip.

Let them all go, the losers!
It's a relief to see Sloth's
fat ass go out the door.
But stick around. I have a story

that not everyone appreciates—
about the special satisfaction
of staying on board as the last
grubby lifeboat pushes away.

DEAL WITH THE DEVIL

The bargain was that he would recollect
each moment of his life entirely—
every touch and taste, no detail lost.

The past would shine forth, not in blinding flashes
but meaningfully the way that music moves,
making a pattern out of every note.

The price was that he had a single year
to contemplate the secrets of his life
before the memories vanished utterly.

"It's a fair deal," the Devil said. "A life
in payment for a life. You won't want more.
Trust me—for most lives, twice is once too often."

"My friend, I'd have your soul in any case.
I've made this offer for my own amusement.
The artist is my favorite customer."

Oddly enough, he did believe the demon.
What point was there revisiting the past?
Why enter that gray Garden of Medusa

To wander through its mute memorials?
Better to let the rain pit, and the years
Erode those granite visages. And yet . . .

He hungered for the stones of memory.
It was the pain itself that he was after
not to alleviate but to perfect—

The delectation of his own damnation—
to earn the blessings of oblivion.
Smiling at Lucifer, he signed his name.

MEDITATION ON A LINE FROM NOVALIS

Wo gehen wir denn hin? Immer nach Hause.

—NOVALIS

When his beloved Sophie died, Novalis
Lay by her grave and wept himself to sleep.
On the third night she met him in a dream.
He woke transformed, longing for the last trance,
"When sleep shall be without waking." Therein,
Observed one critic, "lies his originality"—
Death was not tragedy but a romance.
Where are we going? Home, always back home.

He rarely finished any piece of writing—
"The urge toward perfection is a disease."
Whether through genius or incompetence,
His fragments blur together—but into what?
Not quite philosophy or even art,
But the disclosure of some primal secret.
"Love is the final purpose of the world."
Where are we going? Home, always back home.

"Our life is not a dream but must become one."
He left philosophy to study mining
And prospered in the work. He wrote at night
Drafting out stories that refused to end.
He died at twenty-eight. Schelling kept watch
Beside the poet's sickbed, marveling
How joyfully he contemplated death.
Where are we going? Home, always back home.

TITLE INDEX TO
MY NEXT BOOK OF POEMS

· V ·

STORIES

THE ROOM UPSTAIRS

Come over to the window for a moment—
I want to show you something. Do you see
The one hill without trees? The dust-brown one
Above the highway? That's how it all looked
When I first came—no watered lawns or trees,
Just open desert, pale green in the winter,
Then brown and empty till the end of fall.

I never look in mirrors anymore,
Or if I do, I just stare at the tie
I'm knotting, and it's easy to pretend
I haven't changed. But how can I ignore
The way these hills were cut up into houses?
I always thought the desert would outlive me.

How did I get started on this subject?
I'm really not as morbid as I sound.
We hardly know each other, but I think
You'll like it here—the college isn't far,
And this old house, like me, still has its charms.
I chose the site myself and drew the plans—
A modern house, all open glass and stone,
The rooms squared off and cleared of memory.
No wonder Mother hated the idea.
I had to wait until she died to build.
It was her money after all.

                No,
I never married, never had the time
Or inclination to. Still, getting older,
One wonders . . . not so much about a wife—
No mystery there—but about a son.
I always looked for one among my students

And found too many. Never look for what
You truly want. It comes too easily,
And then you never value it enough—
Until it's gone—gone like these empty hills
And all the years I spent ignoring them.

There was a boy who lived here years ago—
Named David—a clever, handsome boy
Who thought he was a poet. That was back
When I still dreamed of writing. We were both
So full of dreams. He was a student here—
In those rare moments when he chose to study—
But climbing was the only thing he cared for.
It's strange how clearly I remember him.
He lived here off and on almost two years—
In the same room that you are moving into.
You'll like the room. David always did.

Once during a vacation he went off
With friends to climb El Capitan. They took
A girl with them. But it's no easy thing
To climb three thousand feet of granite,
And halfway up, she froze, balanced on a ledge.
They nearly killed themselves to get her down.
At one point David had to wedge himself
Into a crevice, tie down to a rock,
And lower her by rope to another ledge.
When it was over, they were furious.
They drove her back, and he
Surprised me, coming here instead of home.

His clothes were torn, his hands and face cut up.
I went upstairs for bandages, but he
Wanted to shower first. When he called me in,
I watched him standing in the steamy bathroom—
His naked body shining from the water—
Carefully drying himself with a towel.
Then suddenly he threw it down and showed me
Where the ropes had cut into his skin.
It looked as if he had been branded,
Wounds deep enough to hide your fingers in.
I felt like holding him but couldn't bear it.
I helped him into bed and spent the night
Sitting in this room, too upset to sleep.
And on the morning after he drove home.

He graduated just a few months later,
And then went off to Europe where he wrote me
Mainly about beer halls and mountain trips.
I wrote that they would be the death of him.
That spring his mother phoned me when he fell.
I wonder if you know how strange it feels
When someone so much younger than you dies?
And, if I tell you something, will you not
Repeat it? It is something I don't understand.

The night he died I had a dream. I dreamt
That suddenly the room was filled with light,
Not blinding but the soft whiteness that you see
When heavy snow is falling in the morning,
And I awoke to see him standing here,
Waiting in the doorway, his arms outstretched.
"I've come back to you," he said. "Look at me.
Let me show you what I've done for you."

And only then I saw his skin was bruised,
Torn in places, crossed with deep red welts,
But this time everywhere—as if his veins
Had pushed up to the surface and spilled out.
And there was nothing in his body now,
Nothing but the voice that spoke to me,
And this cold white light pouring through the room.

I stared at him. His skin was bright and pale.
"Why are you doing this to me?" I asked.
"Please, go away."
                                "But I've come back to you.
I'm cold. Just hold me. I'm so very cold."

What else could I have done but hold him there?
I took him in my arms—he was so light—
And held him in the doorway listening.
Nothing else was said or lost it seemed.
We waited there while it grew dark again,
And he grew lighter, slipping silently away
Like snow between my fingers, and was gone.

That's all there is to say. I can't explain it,
And now I'm sorry to have bored you so.
It's getting late. You know the way upstairs.
But no, of course not. Let me show you to your room.

COUNTING THE CHILDREN

I.

"This must have been her bedroom, Mr. Choi.
It's hard to tell. The only other time
I came back here was when I found her body."

Neither of us belonged there. She lived next door.
I was the accountant sent out by the State
To take an inventory of the house.

When someone wealthy dies without a will,
The court sends me to audit the estate.
They know that strangers trust a man who listens.

The neighbor led me down an unlit hall.
We came up to a double door and stopped.
She whispered as if someone else were near.

"She used to wander around town at night
And rifle through the trash. We all knew that.
But what we didn't know about was *them*."

She stepped inside and fumbled for a switch.
It didn't work, but light leaked through the curtains.
"Come in," she said. "I want to show you hell."

I walked into a room of wooden shelves
Stretching from floor to ceiling, wall to wall,
With smaller shelves arranged along the center.

A crowd of faces looked up silently.
Shoulder to shoulder, standing all in rows,
Hundreds of dolls were lining every wall.

Not a collection anyone would want—
Just ordinary dolls salvaged from the trash
With dozens of each kind all set together.

Some battered, others missing arms and legs,
Shelf after shelf of the same dusty stare
As if despair could be assuaged by order.

They looked like sisters huddling in the dark,
Forgotten brides abandoned at the altar,
Their veils turned yellow, dresses stiff and soiled.

Rows of discarded little girls and babies—
Some naked, others dressed for play—they wore
Whatever lives their owners left them in.

Where were the children who promised them love?
The small, caressing hands, the lips which whispered
Secrets in the dark? Once they were woken,

Each by name. Now they have become each other—
Anonymous except for injury,
The beautiful and headless side by side.

Was this where all lost childhoods go? These dim
Abandoned rooms, these crude arrangements staged
For settled dust and shadow, left to prove

That all affection is outgrown, or show
The uniformity of our desire?
How dismal someone else's joy can be.

I stood between the speechless shelves and knew
Dust has a million lives, the heart has one.
I turned away and started my report.

II.

That night I dreamt of working on a ledger,
A book so large it stretched across my desk,
Thousands of numbers running down each page.

I knew I had to settle the account,
Yet as I tried to calculate the total,
The numbers started slipping down the page,

Suddenly breaking up like Scrabble letters
Brushed into a box to end a game,
Each strained-for word uncoupled back to nil.

But as I tried to add them back together
And hold each number on the thin green line
Where it belonged, I realized that now

Nothing I did would ever fit together.
In my hands even $2 + 2 + 2$
No longer equaled anything at all.

And then I saw my father there beside me.
He asked me why I couldn't find the sum.
He held my daughter crying in his arms.

My family stood behind him in a row,
Uncles and aunts, cousins I'd never seen,
My grandparents from China and their parents,

All of my family, living and dead,
A line that stretched as far as I could see.
Even the strangers called to me by name.

And now I saw I wasn't at my desk
But working on the coffin of my daughter,
And she would die unless I found the sum.

But I had lost too many of the numbers.
They tumbled to the floor and blazed on fire.
I saw the dolls then—screaming in the flames.

III.

When I awoke, I sat up straight in bed.
The sweaty sheet was twisted in my hands.
My heart was pounding. Had I really screamed?

But no, my wife was still asleep beside me.
I got up quietly and found my robe,
Knowing I couldn't fall asleep again.

Then groping down the unlit hall, I saw
A soft-edged light beneath my daughter's door.
It was the night-light plugged in by her bed.

And I remembered when she was a baby,
How often I would get up in the night
And creep into that room to watch her sleep.

I never told my wife how many times
I came to check each night—or that I was
Always afraid of what I might discover.

I felt so helpless standing by her crib,
Watching the quiet motions of her breath
In the half-darkness of the faint night-light.

How delicate this vessel in our care,
This gentle soul we summoned to the world,
A life we treasured but could not protect.

This was the terror I could not confess—
Not even to my wife—and it was the joy
My daughter had no words to understand.

So standing at my pointless watch each night
In the bare nursery we had improvised,
I learned the loneliness that we call love.

IV.

But I gave up those vigils years ago.
My daughter's seven now, and I don't worry—
At least no more than any father does.

But waking up last night after the dream,
Trembling in the hall, looking at her door,
I let myself be drawn into her room.

She was asleep—the blankets softly rising
And falling with each breath, the faint light tracing
The sleek unfoldings of her long black hair.

Then suddenly I felt myself go numb.
And though you won't believe that an accountant
Can have a vision, I will tell you mine.

Each of us thinks our own child beautiful,
But watching her and marveling at the sheer
Smoothness of skin without a scar or blemish,

I saw beyond my daughter to all children,
And, though elated, still I felt confused
Because I wondered why I never sensed

That thrill of joy when looking at adults
No matter how refined or beautiful,
Why lust or envy always intervened.

There is no *tabula rasa* for the soul.
Each spirit, be it infant, bird or flower,
Comes to the world perfected and complete,

And only time proves its unraveling.
But I'm digressing from my point, my vision.
What I meant to say is merely this:

What if completion comes only in beginnings?
The naked tree exploding into flower?
And all our prim assumptions about time

Prove wrong? What if we cannot read the future
Because our destiny moves back in time,
And only memory speaks prophetically?

We long for immortality, a soul
To rise up flaming from the body's dust.
I know that it exists. I felt it there,

Perfect and eternal in the way
That only numbers are, intangible but real,
Infinitely divisible yet whole.

But we do not possess it in ourselves.
We die, and it abides, and we are one
With all our ancestors, while it divides

Over and over, common to us all,
The ancient face returning in the child,
The distant arms embracing us, the salt

Of our blind origins filling our veins.
I stood confused beside my daughter's bed
Surprised to find the room around me dim.

Then glancing at the bookshelf in the corner,
I saw she'd lined her dolls up in a row.
Three little girls were sitting in the dark.

Their sharp glass eyes surveyed me with contempt.
They recognized me only as a rival,
The one whose world would keep no place for them.

I felt like holding them tight in my arms,
Promising I would never let them go,
But they would trust no promises of mine.

I feared that if I touched one, it would scream.

HOMECOMING

I.

I watched your headlights coming up the drive
and thought, "Thank God, it's over." Do you know
I waited up all night for you—with only
the bugs for company? I tried to watch them
beating their wings against the windowpanes
but only saw my own face staring back,
blurry and bodiless against the black.
Mostly I passed the time remembering
what it was like to grow up in this house.

This little parlor hasn't changed a bit
in twenty years. Those china figurines
along the mantelpiece, the ivory fan,
the green silk pillows puffed up on the couch
were sitting in exactly the same place
when I first came. And that pathetic print
of Jesus smiling by the telephone—
even the music in the piano stool.
These things should have been thrown away by now
or put up in the attic and forgotten.

But you aren't interested in family heirlooms.
The only reason that you're here is me.
I won't resist. I'm ready to go back.
Tomorrow you'll be heroes in the paper—
KILLER NABBED AT FOSTER MOTHER'S HOME.
But first look in the kitchen. No need to rush.

II.

She raised me, but she wasn't family.
I don't know how she first got custody,
except that no one really wanted me.
My father disappeared when I was three.
I don't remember him. A few years later
my mother took off, too. After she left
I saw her only once—by accident—
at the State Fair one Sunday afternoon
when I was twelve. I went without permission.
I should have been attending Bible School
to find salvation over milk and cookies,
but I had sneaked away. I couldn't stand
another dreary day of Jesus. I knew
there would be hell to pay when I got home.
Still I was happy, wandering through the booths,
drunk with the noise, the music, and the rides,
not feeling lonely anymore but merged
into the joyful crowds who didn't care
that it was Sunday. Moving in their midst,
for once I felt I wasn't different,
that we all shared a common world of grace
where simple daylight poured down happiness.

Then suddenly I saw her at a booth—
my mother—talking to some man, and she
was holding a stuffed animal they'd won,
chatting with it in the sort of baby talk
that lovers use. At first I wasn't sure
if it was her. I started to call out.
She noticed then that I was watching her.

And for an instant we stood face to face.
I knew from pictures it was her. And she
paused for a moment, staring absently.
A puzzled look, a moment's hesitation,
and then she winked at me—the intimacy
of strangers at a summer fair—and smiled
without the slightest trace of recognition.
I turned and ran the whole way home.
That evening when the old bitch paddled me
for missing church, for once I didn't mind.

III.

God didn't care. He saw where I belonged.
She told me years ago how everyone
would either go to Heaven or to Hell.
God knew it all, and nothing you could do
would make a difference. I asked her how
a person knew where he was chosen for.
She said, "A person always knows inside."
She asked me suddenly—for the first time—
if I were saved. I couldn't give an answer.
"Look in your heart," she told me. "Look for Jesus."

All night I lay in bed and thought about it.
I tried to pray, but mostly I just kept
imagining my heart, how dry it was
and empty like a shell that long ago
someone had picked up sparkling from the surf.
But now it lies in a cluttered dresser drawer
where no one ever touches it again.

And if you ever held it to your ear,
you wouldn't hear the crash of ocean waves.
All you would feel is the harshness of bone.
All you would hear is a hush of loneliness
so small that you could hold it in your hand.

That night I knew that I would go to Hell,
and it would be a place just like my room—
dark, suffocating, with its door shut tight,
and even if my mother were there too,
she wouldn't find me. I'd always be alone.

IV.

The next night I left home. I walked for miles
through fields and farmland without any aim.
It was so dark I couldn't see my way.
Then pushing through a cornfield, suddenly
I tripped and slid into some kind of hole.
I clutched the muddy walls to break my fall.
They crumbled at my weight. Each time I tried
to right myself I slipped and fell again.
Stuck ankle-deep in mud, I screamed for help,
struggling in darkness, unable to escape.

Finally I lay there panting at the bottom.
It seemed so deep I didn't try again,
and, absolutely sure that I would die there,
I fell asleep, still glad that I'd left home.

And I remember waking up that morning
in a deep ditch beside a cornfield. I
was hungry, cold. My clothes were caked with mud.
The first thing that I noticed was a crow
perched right above me on the ditch's edge,
blinking and cawing at the murky sky.
I lay there shaking, stupidly afraid
the bird would swoop and blind me with his claws.
Trying to keep still, holding my breath,
I watched him pacing back and forth while slowly
the cool green daylight filtered through the corn.

I finally summoned courage to stand up,
and—just like that—the startled bird flapped off.
At first I was embarrassed. How had I
become so terrified of that small creature?
But then I had to laugh. I realized
how many of the things I feared in life
were likely just as much afraid of me.
I knew I could climb out then, and I did—
digging myself a sort of runway up.
Gasping for breath, I knelt down in the field
between the tall straight rows of sunlit corn
and swore I'd never be afraid again.

They found me the next day and brought me home.
That's when I started getting into trouble.
My teachers always wondered why a kid
as smart as me would lie so shamelessly
or pick a fight for no apparent reason.
She wondered, too—as if intelligence
was ever any guarantee of goodness.

V.

I used to read at night back in my room.
I liked adventure stories most of all
and books about the War—*To Hell and Back,
The Death March at Bataan.* You know the sort.
There weren't more than a dozen books at home,
mainly the Bible and religious crap,
but back in town there was a library.

The books I liked the best I used to steal.
I filled my room with them—*Pellucidar,
The Dunwich Horror, Master of the World,
Robur the Conqueror, Tarzan the Untamed.*
I didn't want them read by anyone but me—
not that the folks I knew were in much danger
of opening a book which had no pictures.

The more I read the more I realized
that power was the only thing that mattered.
The weak made rules to penalize the strong,
but if the strong refused to be afraid,
they always found another way to win.

Sometimes when she dozed off, I'd slip outside
and head off through the trees behind the house.
She said these woods had been a pasture once,
but now a second growth of scruffy pine
covered the fields as far as you could see.
I had a special hiding place back there.

Near the foundations of a ruined farmhouse
there was a boarded-up old well. I'd pried
a couple of planks loose covering it.
If I came there at noon, I could look down
and see the deep black sparkle of the water
framed by the darkness of the earthen walls.
At night it was an emptiness of must
and fading echoes that could swallow up
a falling match before it reached the bottom.
Sometimes I'd stretch along beside it dreaming.

I knew there was a boy who'd fallen there.
His family had boarded up the well
and moved away to let the trees reclaim
the fields they'd spent so many years to clear.
I wondered if they'd ever found the body
or if it floated there beneath the surface,
the features bloated like a sopping sponge,
the skin as black as the surrounding earth.

I didn't mention it to anyone.
This was my place. I didn't want it spoiled.
Most people are too weak to keep a secret,
but I knew knowledge gives a person power.
I came there every evening—or at least
whenever I could sneak away from her.

One night I started whispering down the well.
What was it like, I asked him, to be dead?
What was there left without your family,
your home, your friends, even your name forgotten,
the light shut out, the moist earth pressing round?

Of course he didn't answer me. The dead
never do. Not him. Not even Jesus.
Only a razor's edge of moonlight gleamed,
silent at the bottom of the well.

I realized that if he could return,
if he could rise again through the dark shaft
and stand there in the sun, breathing the air,
what use would all our morals be to him?
Death leaves an emptiness that words can't fill.
No, he would seize whatever things he wanted,
and what would guilt or honesty or love
matter to him now? Coming from the dead,
he would be something more or less than human,
something as cruel and hungry as a wolf.

How was I any different from him?
I came to death each day and sat beside it.
I breathed its musty odor in my lungs.
That was the night that I was born again,
not out of death, but into it—with him,
my poor unwitting savior in the well.
If I could only become strong enough,
I could do anything. I simply had
to tear away the comfortable lies,
the soft morality—the way a snake
sloughs skin when it becomes too small, the way
a wolf cub sheds its milkteeth for its fangs.

The next day when I saw a neighbor's dog
sniffing around the well, I called him over.
I let him nuzzle me, then slit his throat.
I stuffed him full of rocks and threw him in.

I wanted to be sick, but I stayed strong.
Later I killed a cat and then another dog,
and when I heard two neighbors talk about
keeping their kids and pets inside at night
because a wolf had come down from the hills,
I had to smile. My new life had begun.

I started pulling petty robberies,
spaced months apart at first but then more often.
I never got caught though, except by her.
I'd come home late at night, and there she'd be
staring at me, so pious, old, and ugly—
although she didn't guess the half of it.
So things went on like that until one night
they caught me cold, and I still had the gun.

VI.

In prison everyone's a little crazy—
nothing to do and lots of time to do it.
So soon you either fasten on some memory
or lose your mind. Most guys just choose a woman
or a special place, but who knows what it takes
to make one thing stick in your mind for years?
Some people there, who barely talked outside,
would ramble on for hours about Sue
or Laurie Jean, Lynette or dear old Mama.
I knew a fellow who talked all day long
about some Friday night five years before
when he'd gone drinking with his older brothers.
He sat there trying to remember it,
putting each scrap exactly in its place—

the car, the burger joint, the brand of beer.
And when no one would listen anymore,
he sat at dinner by himself and drew
street maps of his hometown on paper napkins,
carefully marking out the route they traveled.
Madness makes storytellers of us all.

I was no different. Think of it this way:
I lay there in my cell for seven years
and stared up at a window blank with sky,
day after day when nothing came in view.
My cell was littered with unfinished books.
The chaplain always complimented me
for reading, but he didn't understand.
The stories didn't matter anymore.
I grew to hate them. Writers lie too much.
They offer an escape which seems so real,
but when you're finished, nothing ever changes.
The things I wanted couldn't come from books.

I used to make up games to pass the time.
My favorite was called Roommates. I'd catch
a horsefly or a cockroach in a jar—
that would be roommate number one—and then
I'd look behind the toilet for a spider.
I'd drop him in the jar and see what happened.
I liked to watch the roommates get acquainted.
Know what I learned? That spiders always win.

At night I tried to keep myself from screaming.
I'd lie there listening to the toilets flush,
the bedposts scrape the floor, the yard dogs howl,

the guards who shuffled down the corridors,
the fellow in the next cell jerking off.
I had to think of something to keep sane,
and so I thought of her, of everything
she did for me, of everything she said.
I looked into my heart and heard a voice.
It told me what I must have known for years.

VII.

When they escape, most guys head straight for town,
steal anything they can, get drunk, get laid,
and then get caught. They don't know what they want.
I knew exactly why I'd risked my neck.

I made it quite a distance before daybreak,
but, when the light came up, I started shaking.
I'd killed a guard the night before. I'd scaled
a barbwire fence that sliced up both my hands
and slithered through a slime-wet sewage pipe.
But I had planned that part back in my cell.
The thing I hadn't counted on was sunlight—
the sun and open spaces . . . there were no walls!
I had forgotten what the world was like.

I started crying. Can you picture me
standing there stunned and squinting like a mole
someone had flushed out of the ground to kill?
What a damn fool I was—stumbling around
in prison workclothes on an open road.
I tried to hitch a ride, and right away

a lady picked me up. She said I looked
just like her son in Tulsa. She talked a lot.
There's always someone stupider than you.
I ditched the car at nightfall in a field,
and walked the six miles home. I knew the way.

VIII.

I walked up to the house, then went around.
The front door was for company, not me.
I went up to the kitchen porch and knocked.
I was afraid that she'd look old and sick,
that I would lose my nerve, but then she answered,
looking the same and acting as if she
were not at all surprised to see me there.

She looked the same, and yet I realized
that moment how I had forgotten all
the features of her face. More likely I
had never really noticed them at all—
her freckled skin, the bump along her nose,
the narrow tight-drawn lips which formed a smile
that I had seen before, not just on her.
It was the smile I greeted in the mirror.
I never knew till then where I had learned it.
How strange the people we are closest to
remain almost invisible to us
until we leave them. Then, on our return,
we recognize the faces in our dreams.

I saw her calmly now. And what I saw
was an old woman close enough to death.
How pointless my revenge seemed in that moment.
Nothing could redeem the past—or me.
I had no right to come and stand in judgment.

IX.

These thoughts took just a moment, then I heard
"I'll set another place for you at supper."
She had a way about her, see? A way
of putting everyone back in their place,
no matter who they were or what they wanted.
She knew that she had won. And didn't care.

That's when I noticed she had set three places.
Reading the question on my face, she said,
"I have another boy who lives here now."
I told her that I wanted to wash up,
but went instead back to the extra bedroom,
and walked right in.

                      I guess I must have scared him.
He was a scrawny kid with short red hair,
not more than twelve with narrow mousy eyes.
He sat there on the rug, his mouth half-open,
his baseball cards laid out across the floor.

I knew the room. It hadn't changed at all.
The blistered paint, the battered bed and desk
still moaned about the cost of charity.

He crouched there looking at me silently.
Watching him tense, I knew how many times
that angry men had come to him before.
He had the wisdom of the unloved child
who knew he had been damned by being born.

I closed the door behind me. Frantically
he gathered up his cards to stash away.
They must have seemed more precious than his life.
As I came close, I didn't say a word
but took the cash I'd stolen from the guard
and held it out, "Take this and walk to town."
He knew that money never comes for free.
He took it anyway and slipped outside.

I walked back to the kitchen quietly
and saw her busy working at the sink.
She must have heard me come into the room,
but wouldn't turn to look me in the face.
And I came up behind her all at once.
Then it was over—over just like that.

I felt a sudden tremor of delight,
a happiness that went beyond my body
as if the walls around me had collapsed,
and a small dark room where I had been confined
had been amazingly transformed by light.
Radiant and invincible, I knew
I was the source of energy, and all
the jails and sheriffs could not hold me back.
I had stayed strong. Finally, I was free.

But as I stood there gloating, gradually
the darkness and the walls closed in again.
Sensing the power melting from my arms,
I realized the energy I felt
was just adrenaline—the phony high
that violence unleashes in your blood.
I saw her body lying on the floor
and knew that we would always be together.
All I could do was wait for the police.
I had come home, and there was no escape.

HAUNTED

"I don't believe in ghosts," he said. "Such nonsense.
But years ago I actually saw one."
He seemed quite serious, and so I asked.

It happened almost forty years ago.
The world was different then—not just for ghosts—
slower, less frantic. You're too young to know
life without cell phones, laptops, satellite.
You didn't bring the world with you everywhere.
Out in the country, you were quite alone.

I was in love with Mara then, if love
is the right word for that particular
delusion. We were young. We thought we could
create a life made only of peak moments.
We laughed. We drank. We argued and made love.
Our battles were Homeric—not Homer's heroes
but his gods, petty, arrogant Olympians
thundering in their egotistic rage.

Mara was brilliant, beautiful, refined.
She'd walk into a room dressed for the evening,
and I would lose a breath. She seemed to shine
as movie stars shine, made only of light.
And did I mention she was rich? And cruel?

Do you know what it's like to be in love
with someone bad? Not simply bad for you,
but slightly evil? You have to decide
either to be the victim or accomplice.
I'm not the victim type. That's what she liked.

I envied her sublime self-confidence.
She could freeze someone with a single sentence,
too witty to be rude but deeply wounding,
impossible to deflect or forget.
If I sound slightly bitter, please understand,
it is myself I now despise, not Mara.
She simply recognized what I desired.

Her uncle owned a house up in the Berkshires,
not just a summer house, a country manor,
three stories high with attics, basement, turrets,
surrounded by great lawns and sunken gardens,
hundreds of wooded acres whispering wealth.

We came up for a few days in late autumn,
driving through bare woods under a gray sky,
the landscape still, no birds, barely a breeze,
hushed as the hour after heavy snowfall.

The house had been vacated since September.
I had imagined it as dark and gothic,
cloaked in shadow like something out of Lovecraft,
but the decor was opulently cozy,
a proper refuge for a Robber Baron,
stuffed with *objets* to certify his status,
though slightly shabby from a century's use.

The art was grand, authentic, second rate.
Florentine bronzes, Belgian tapestries,
carved stonework pried from bankrupt Tudor manors,
and landscapes by the minor Barbizons.
Nothing quite fit together. I suspect

sumptuous excess was the desired effect,
a joyful shout to celebrate success—
good taste be damned—let's just indulge ourselves
and revel like a child who greets his playmates
by emptying his toy chest on the floor.
What fun is wealth if no one notices?
Mara seemed to think so. What did I know?
I'd never seen the rich up close before.

While Mara showered, I explored the cellars,
searching a maze of mildewed storage rooms
until I found a faux medieval door,
flanked by a pair of somber wooden saints.
You should have seen the wine her uncle owned—
six vaulted rooms stocked with the great estates,
bin after bin of legendary names,
Château Margaux, Latour, Lafite-Rothschild,
a prodigal accumulation formed
on such a scale he could have entertained
Napoleon and half his *Grande Armée*.

I chose two bottles of pre-war Petrus
That probably cost as much as my month's rent.
Clutching their dusty necks, I closed the door,
And told the saints, "I could get used to this."
They didn't condescend to give an answer.

That night we drank in the high paneled library,
a great inferno blazing in the fireplace.
Naked Diana stood in tapestry
above us on the wall. Below her, Mara,
stylishly overdressed, refilled our glasses.

Resplendently the room reminded us
that beauty always bears a heavy price.
White tiger skins lay stretched across the floor.
Martyred Sebastian twisted on a pedestal.
Even the dusty books were bound in leather.

Mara loved having me as audience.
She sat there, half illumined by the fire
and half in shadow, spinning out long stories.
They were as fine as anything in books.
No, they were better because they were true.

She was a connoisseur of *Schadenfreude*
and was especially wicked in describing
her former lovers—imitating them,
cataloguing their signature stupidities,
and relishing their subsequent misfortunes.
(I'm surely in her repertory now.)

At first I was embarrassed by her candor.
I felt more like a confidant than lover,
but gradually I understood the motive—
even she needed someone to impress.
Life was a contest. Mara was a champion.
What good was winning if no one noticed?

Of course, that night we drank too much and argued.
She strode off, slamming doors theatrically.
I sat still, slowly finishing my drink,
feigning indifference—just as she would have—
and then went to the other wing to sleep.
Let her find me, I thought. Let her apologize.
She won't like sleeping in this house alone.

The room was cold, and I was too annoyed
to fall asleep. I stretched out on the bed,
still wearing all my clothes, and tried to read.
Believe it or not, the book was Shakespeare's sonnets.
What sweeter text for wounded vanity?
Farewell, thou art too dear for my possessing.
I'd found an old edition in the library,
and from sheer spitefulness I'd stolen it.
That night each poem seemed written just for me.
What is your substance, whereof are you made,
That millions of strange shadows on you tend?

I hope this explanation makes it clear
I wasn't sleeping when I saw her enter—
Mara, I thought, mad at being ignored,
coming to make a scene. But, no, it was
a handsome woman in her early forties.
I thought she might have been a housekeeper
come in from town to check up on the place,
but why was she so elegantly dressed?

I started to explain why I was there.
She didn't seem to hear and turned away.
Could she be deaf? I didn't want to scare her.
Something was wrong. I couldn't see her clearly.
She seemed at once herself and her own reflection
shimmering on the surface of clear water
where fleeting shadows twisted in the depths.

I found it hard admitting what I saw.
She seemed to be a ghost, though that sounds crazy.
Oddly, I wasn't scared—just full of wonder,
watching this thing I knew could not exist,
this woman standing by her dressing table,
translucent, insubstantial, but still there,
and utterly oblivious of me.
First to be haunted, then to be ignored!

Her back toward me, she started to undress.
Now I was panicked and embarrassed both.
I spoke much louder. She made no response.
Now wearing only a long silk chemise,
she turned toward me, still strangely indistinct,
the fabric undulating, as if alive.
I felt her eyes appraise me, and I sat
half paralyzed as she approached the bed.

Here I was face to face with a dead soul,
some entity regathered from the dust,
returned like Lazarus from the silent tomb,
whose mere existence, right before my eyes,
confounded my belief there could not be
an afterlife. Think what this meeting represented—
a skeptic witnessing the unexplained.

I could have learned the secrets of the dead
if there are any secrets, which I doubt.
So how did I address this revenant,
this traveler from the undiscovered country,
who stared at me with dark, unblinking eyes?
I caught my breath, got on my feet, and said—
nothing at all. The words stuck in my throat.

We stood there face to face, inches apart.
Her pale skin shined like a window catching sunlight,
both bright and clear, but chilling to the touch.
She stared at me with undisguised contempt,
and then she whispered, almost in a hiss,
"You don't belong here. No, you don't belong here."
She slowly reached to touch me, and I ran
leaving behind both Shakespeare and my shoes.

Mara was still awake when I arrived.
The lamp was on. The fireplace ablaze.
And she stretched naked under satin sheets.
"So, you've come back?" she yawned with mock ennui,
then added with a smirk, "You weren't gone long."
I didn't say a word of what I'd seen.

We used to sleep in one another's arms,
our two slim bodies interlaced like hands.
That night I held her, feeling our hearts beat—
first hers, then mine—always out of sync,
and in the dark I thought, *I don't belong here,*
I don't belong here. Slipping out of bed,
I quickly dressed, and what I couldn't wear
I left behind—the clothes, the books, the camera,
no longer mine. What a surprise to first feel
the liberations of divestiture.

I moved with such new lightness down the stairs,
watched by mute saints and marble goddesses.
Then out the door. I closed it quietly.
The lock clicked shut. Good-bye to both my ghosts.

I made it to the county road by dawn
and hitched a ride on an old dairy truck.
"What happened to your shoes?" the driver said.
"No, better yet, don't tell me. Just get in."

I climbed in, and one road led to another.
And now I'm in your bar. That's probably not
the story you expected from a monk,
delivering brandy from the monastery.
Not all of us began as altar boys.

I've been there fifteen years. I like the drill—
Poverty, Chastity, and Growing Grapes.
The archbishop calls my port a miracle.
Don't tell His Grace, but I still doubt there is
an afterlife. That's not why I stay there.
This is the life I didn't want to waste.

STYLE

I.

Just look at me. Isn't it obvious?
I have no style. I'm just a human blur.
On me expensive clothes look second-hand.
They droop or sag. The color's never right.
I wear the wrong apparel to the party.
I pick the dullest item on the menu.
Each haircut brings some new humiliation.

That's why I always loved to visit Tom.
He had the perfect sense for what was perfect.
He never wore a sports coat or a shirt
That didn't seem exactly right—not just
For him but for the time, the place, the people.
It wasn't just his clothes, but how he smiled
Or shook your hand or listened to a joke.

I've never seen a person comparable,
Except in movies of a certain era,
The sort where Cary Grant casually enters
In clothes of such exquisite tailoring
The cameras caress him like a lover,
Or Garbo lifts a cocktail to her lips
So that you, sitting in the dark, can taste
A dozen heartbreaks in a single gesture.

I know exactly what you're thinking now—
My story and my friend seem superficial.
You don't take people like us seriously,
Though every day you pass us on the street.
What does style matter? Quite a lot, I say.

Style isn't fashion. It's knowing who you are
And how you hold yourself up to the world.
It's the clear surface that lets you see the depths.

I wake up many mornings full of dread,
Knowing my life is not what I intended.
Just like my clothes, it doesn't really fit.
(What was it I intended anyway?)
Most lives consist of choosing the wrong things.
We try to compensate by choosing more,
As if sheer mass bestowed integrity.

II.

We met in college. Never closest friends,
We always stayed in touch. I'll never know
Just what he saw in me—perhaps an audience.
No, that's unfair. I think it was pure kindness.
I stumbled through life losing jobs and girls,
Wasting the little money that I made.

Tom was a golden boy. While others climbed,
He took flight. His success was existential:
It wasn't what he did; he simply was
The way he was, which is to say, he was
Exactly what the business world wanted.

At thirty-two he started his own firm.
At thirty-five he took the venture public.
He prospered like one chosen by the gods.
His corner office seemed built on a cloud—
With miles of open sky and bright blue water

Shining through the glass walls above the bay.
So effortless and absolute his triumph,
Who could have guessed the way the story ended?

Tom put me on the list for all his parties.
I had no dignity. I always went,
Eager and underdressed. He had the trick
Of going to the limits of delight
While never overstepping to excess.

He booked the most astonishing locations—
The Rainbow Room at Rockefeller Center,
The Hall of the Great Whale, the Stock Exchange,
And the Egyptian Temple at the Met.
He turned each place into a sort of stage.

These parties made me feel as if I'd walked
Into the secret movie in my mind
Where I'm the star, and everything is bright,
Glamorous, and romantic—even me.

Tom dated a succession of tall beauties.
And then came Eden. I can't be objective
In any way about her. She was perfect—
Beautiful, elegant, intelligent.
I want to say *divine*—probably because
The first time that I saw her she was bathed
In golden light against a colonnade
At the Met's temple of the goddess Isis.
The vision was purely theatrical—
Tom's party-planners doing their paid magic.
But even tricks bestow a sense of wonder.

I watched him climb the temple steps to join her.
They were magnificent, and utterly
Asexual. They seemed like seraphim
Who had transcended bodily desire.
Their love, so eminently evident,
Expressed in warmth and courteous attention.
I was a caveman staring at the stars.

III.

After they married, I saw less of Tom—
The occasional lunch or cocktail party.
Eden was always gracious. So was he,
But his success took all his time to manage,
Not just his business but his boards and charities.

Then suddenly the invitations stopped.
I didn't feel insulted or surprised.
I had expected such a break for years.
I barely had a life. Tom had it all.

Later I read his firm had been shut down.
I figured Tom had cashed out and retired,
Still young enough to sail around the world,
Climb Everest, or whatever it is
Ex-CEOs do with their portfolios—
An afterlife of private jets and yacht clubs.

One night I found myself at the St. Regis.
I'd made another unsuccessful pitch
Over a dinner I could not afford—

My shabby life about to crash again.
Angry, depressed, I lurched into the bar.
There at a table, by herself, sat Eden.

She wore a silver-sequined evening gown
And held a glass of wine between her hands.
She didn't drink but rolled it back and forth,
Staring at the bright murals on the wall.
Seeing her there gave me a twinge of joy.

"What a surprise to find you here," I said,
Acting as if I came there every night.
"Waiting for Tom?" She barely raised her eyes,
Looking at me as if I were a stranger.
"No," she said, after a pause. "Not for Tom.
There was a benefit upstairs. I needed air."
Then came another pause. "Didn't you know?
Tom and I are not together now."

I probably should have left her at that point,
But I'm not skilled in social situations,
And so I simply blurted out, "What happened?"
She turned the glass around again and told me.

IV.

"About three years ago, Tom became ill.
The doctors couldn't pinpoint what was wrong.
He was in constant pain, but he insisted,
'We won't let this condition slow us down.
It's just another problem to be solved.'
We both knew he was good at solving problems.

But month by month, the symptoms got much worse.
The doctors offered different diagnoses.
They gave him drugs, more drugs, then radiation.
If it had only been the pain, I think
We would have made it through this trial together,
But something unexpected happened to him.

His looks began to change. His face puffed up.
His features thickened, and his hair thinned out.
He didn't look that bad, at least at first,
But he no longer looked at all like Tom.
One morning he stopped going to the office.
He was the one who always closed the deals.
Without him, business slowed, the clients fled.
A few months later Tom shut the place down.

His face kept getting worse. One afternoon
When I came home from work, he left the room.
Shutting the door, he cried, 'Don't look at me!'
I leaned against the door and said I loved him
No matter what he looked like. I see now
What a mistake that was. Later that night
He took the mirrors down in the apartment.
I didn't like it, but I understood.

I hardly saw him after that. He hid
Whenever I was home. A few days later
I saw that all our photographs were gone,
Even our wedding book, all thrown away.
I screamed at him, then cried. I asked him why.
He said, 'I didn't like them anymore.'

Six months ago he simply moved away—
No note, no warning, nothing else was missing,
No clothes, no books, not even his cell phone,
None of the beautiful things we chose together.
I thought he would come back. I waited for him.
I worried that he might have killed himself.
Then a new check came through on his account—
Just for a small amount, but signed by him.
Finally, some detectives tracked him down.
They gave me an address. And so I went.

The taxi took me to a tenement.
Could the address be right? The place was sordid.
I hesitated to get out alone.
I had the driver wait along the curb.
Garbage was piled on both sides of the door.
The corridors were dark and smelled of grease.
How could Tom leave me for this awful place?

I found his door and knocked. There was no answer.
I knocked again, and then I lost control.
I pounded wildly, screaming at the door.
Finally, a voice spoke. His voice. It said,
'The person that you're looking for is gone.
Tom isn't here. Tom isn't anywhere.'
I begged and wept. He wouldn't let me in.
A neighbor came out in his underwear
And stared at me. I felt ashamed and left."

Back in the bar, as Eden told me this,
She started crying, sobbing quietly.
I reached to touch her hand. She pulled away.
Then she looked up at me. Her eyes were blackened,

Smeared from her streaked eyeliner, but they shined
With the intensity of the insane.
"Charlie," she said. "You've got to talk to him.
Tom always said you were his closest friend."

V.

The "sordid" tenement turned out to be
An ordinary place, down on its luck.
Despite the filthy brick facade, it wasn't
Much worse than the apartment where I lived.
His hallway, though, really did stink of grease,
And half the bulbs were burnt out in the stairwell.

I knocked three times, then shouted out my name.
After a pause, I heard the deadbolt turn.
Then a familiar voice responded softly,
"Come in, old friend. I hoped that you would visit."

I walked into a dark and empty room.
Only a folding table and a chair—
The sort of junk you see left on the street.
Piles of old newspapers littered the floor.
Some slats of light leaked through the window blinds.

I did not recognize the man who sat there,
His coarse, flat features or his bloated face.
His hair was gone. One eye was swollen shut.
He was dressed only in a dirty robe.
His body was a leopard skin of bruises.

"Welcome," he said, "to the Kingdom of the Dead.
I wish that I could offer you a chair,
But don't expect good manners from the damned.
I should apologize about the smell,
But once apologies begin, where would I stop?"

"I'm here," I told him, "because Eden asked me."

"I hope you've seen enough to understand
I can't go back. The man I was is dead.
I'm just the fellow waiting for the hearse.
Mentioning Eden only makes it worse.
Even a monster has his vanity.

I left the other man his life intact.
I didn't steal a thing, not even her.
Don't think I wasn't tempted, but why pack
All of the beautiful things you can't take with you?
My new style, as you see, is minimal."

"How can you talk that way about your wife?
This is no time for striking clever poses."

"You seem surprised to find me eloquent.
Being well-spoken is all I have left.
I want to make this conversation matter.
We'll never have a chance to speak again."

"Not if you end up staying here!" I cried.

"I'm glad, " he said, "to hear you speak of endings.
My downfall makes a very shabby story.
Reality has made a botch of it.
First up, then down—no nuance, no panache,
In short, no style. After playing the prince,
I find it difficult to be recast
As Caliban for my farewell performance.
I could endure this suffering or worse
If I could end as something other than
An object of intolerable pity.
The ending is what gives a story meaning.

So let me start my new and last career—
The editor who will revise this story.
If I'm compelled to play the monster's role,
Then let the monster have his grand finale.
Give me a death scene and a juicy speech,
Not a morphine drip in a hospice bed,
Nor a last whimper to a paid attendant.

Report whatever details you see fit.
It might be easier for everyone
To term this denouement an accident.
For me, it is enough that you bear witness.
You always understood my sense of style."

He took a book of matches from his pocket.
Struck one. It flamed. He dropped it on the floor.
The fuel-soaked papers at his feet took fire.
"You'd better go," he said. I backed away.
The inferno had been carefully devised.
The blaze reached out in lines across the room.
As the fire spread, the flames were beautiful.

VI.

"No one knows how the accident occurred.
It happened after I left," I told Eden.
We sat on an immaculate divan
Beneath a David Hockney Swimming Pool.
The windows gave a view of Central Park.

"Tom and I talked about his situation.
He said that he was sorry you had suffered.
He had almost decided to come home.
As I walked out, he stopped me for a moment.
He made me promise I would visit you."

· VI ·

SONGS

THE COUNTRY WIFE

She makes her way through the dark trees
Down to the lake to be alone.
Following their voices on the breeze,
She makes her way. Through the dark trees
The distant stars are all she sees.
They cannot light the way she's gone.
She makes her way through the dark trees
Down to the lake to be alone.

The night reflected on the lake,
The fire of stars changed into water.
She cannot see the winds that break
The night reflected on the lake
But knows they motion for her sake.
These are the choices they have brought her:
The night reflected on the lake,
The fire of stars changed into water.

SONG FOR THE END OF TIME

The hanged man laughs by the garden wall,
And the hands of the clock have stopped at the hour.
The cathedral angels are starting to fall,
And the bells ring themselves in the gothic tower.

Lock up your money and go bolt the door,
And don't dare look yourself in the eye.
Pray on your knees or cry on the floor
Or stare at the stars as they fall from the sky.

You may say that you're sorry for all that you've done,
You may swear on your honor and protest with tears,
But the moon is burning under the sun,
And nothing you do will stop what appears.

THE ARCHBISHOP

For a famous critic

O do not disturb the Archbishop,
Asleep in his ivory chair.
You must send all the workers away,
Though the church is in need of repair.

His Reverence is tired from preaching
To the halt, and the lame, and the blind.
Their spiritual needs are unsubtle,
Their notions of God unrefined.

The Lord washed the feet of His servants.
"The first shall be last," He advised.
The Archbishop's edition of Matthew
Has that troublesome passage revised.

The Archbishop declines to wear glasses,
So his sense of the world grows dim.
He thinks that the crowds at Masses
Have gathered in honor of him.

In the crypt of the limestone cathedral
A friar recopies St. Mark,
A nun serves stew to a novice,
A choirboy sobs in the dark.

While high in the chancery office
His Reverence studies the glass,
Wondering which of his vestments
Would look best at Palm Sunday Mass.

The saints in their weather-stained niches
Weep as the Vespers are read,
And the beggars sleep on the church steps,
And the orphans retire unfed.

On Easter the Lord is arisen
While the Archbishop breakfasts in bed,
And the humble shall find resurrection,
And the dead shall lie down with the dead.

NOSFERATU'S SERENADE

I am the image that darkens your glass,
The shadow that falls wherever you pass.
I am the dream you cannot forget,
The face you remember without having met.

I am the truth that must not be spoken,
The midnight vow that cannot be broken.
I am the bell that tolls out the hours.
I am the fire that warms and devours.

I am the hunger that you have denied,
The ache of desire piercing your side.
I am the sin you have never confessed,
The forbidden hand caressing your breast.

You've heard me inside you speak in your dreams,
Sigh in the ocean, whisper in streams.
I am the future you crave and you fear.
You know what I bring. Now I am here.

(From Nosferatu*)*

MAD SONG

I sailed a ship
In the storm-wracked sea,
And all were drowned
Except for me.
I swam all night
Through death-cold waves
Till my shipmates called
From their sunken graves,
A lucky life for you, lad, a lucky life for you!

I fought through wars
In a barren land
Till none were left
Of my rugged band.
On a field of dead
Only I stood free.
Then a blind crow laughed
From a blasted tree,
A lucky life for you, lad, a lucky life for you!

I scaled a mountain
Of cold sharp stone.
The others fell,
And I climbed alone.
When I reached the top,
The winds were wild,
But a skull at my feet
Looked up and smiled,
A lucky life for you, lad, a lucky life for you!

(*From* Nosferatu)

ALLEY CAT LOVE SONG

Come into the garden, Fred,
For the neighborhood tabby is gone.
Come into the garden, Fred.
I have nothing but my flea collar on,
And the scent of catnip has gone to my head.
I'll wait by the screen door till dawn.

The fireflies court in the sweetgum tree.
The nightjar calls from the pine,
And she seems to say in her rhapsody,
"Oh, mustard-brown Fred, be mine!"
The full moon lights my whiskers afire,
And the fur goes erect on my spine.

I hear the frogs in the muddy lake
Croaking from shore to shore.
They've one swift season to soothe their ache.
In autumn they sing no more.
So ignore me now, and you'll hear my meow
As I scratch all night at the door.

MARKETING DEPARTMENT TRIO

Classical music's
Gotta go.
All the surveys
Tell us so.
Brahms is boring.
Bach is dreary.
Morning drive time
Should be cheery.

Grieg is stale.
Mozart moldy.
Give us this day
Our golden oldie.
Tchaikovsky's pathetic.
Schubert's a nerd.
And once is too much
For Beethoven's Third.

The past is over.
Let's clean house.
Out with Verdi.
Good-bye Strauss.
Curtains for opera.
Unstring that cello.
Make the music
Soft and mellow.

Whether you're driving
Or trying to score,
Lean back, relax,
While our ratings soar.
Mile after mile
Commute with a smile.
So bye-bye Beethoven,
And don't touch that dial!

(From Tony Caruso's Final Broadcast*)*

PITY THE BEAUTIFUL

Pity the beautiful,
the dolls, and the dishes,
the babes with big daddies
granting their wishes.

Pity the pretty boys,
the hunks, and Apollos,
the golden lads whom
success always follows.

The hotties, the knock-outs,
the tens out of ten,
the drop-dead gorgeous,
the great leading men.

Pity the faded,
the bloated, the blowsy,
the paunchy Adonis
whose luck's gone lousy.

Pity the gods,
no longer divine.
Pity the night
the stars lose their shine.

REUNION

This is my past where no one knows me.
These are my friends whom I can't name—
Here in a field where no one chose me,
The faces older, the voices the same.

Why does this stranger rise to greet me?
What is the joke that makes him smile,
As he calls the children together to meet me
Bringing them forward in single file?

I nod pretending to recognize them,
Not knowing exactly what I should say.
Why does my presence seem to surprise them?
Who is the woman who turns away?

Is this my home or an illusion?
The bread on the table smells achingly real.
Must I at last solve my confusion,
Or is confusion all I can feel?

THE HEART OF THE MATTER

The heart of the matter, the ghost of a chance,
A tremor, a fever, an ache in the chest.
The moth and the candle beginning their dance,
A cool white sheet on which nothing will rest.

Come sit beside me. I've waited alone.
What you need to confess I already know.
The scent of your shame is a heavy cologne
That lingers for hours after you go.

The dregs of the bottle, the end of the line,
The laggard, the loser, the last one to know.
The unfinished book, the dead-end sign,
And last summer's garden buried in snow.

COLD SAN FRANCISCO

I shall meet you again in cold San Francisco
On the hillside street overlooking the bay.
We shall go to the house where we buried the years,
Where the door is locked, and we haven't a key.
We'll pause on the steps as the fog burns away,
And the chill waves shimmer in the sun's dim glow,
And we'll gaze down the hill at the bustling piers
Where the gulls shout their hymns to being alive,
And the high-masted boats that we never sailed
Stand poised to explore the innocent blue.
I shall speak your name like a foreign word,
Uncertain what it means, and you—
What will you say in that salt-heavy air
On that bright afternoon that will never arrive?

HOUSEHOLD GODS

Felis catus

The gods of ancient Egypt
Have walked into the room.
While Isis and Osiris
Were sealed inside their tomb,
These sleek divinities escaped
To build their sect anew
And cultivate the worship
Of Christian, Hindu, Jew.

In mystic meditation
The gods their vigil keep.
(Only the foolish heathen
Mistake their bliss for sleep.)
No worldly care can interrupt
Their transcendental state
Of pure incorporality
Beside the heating grate.

Aegyptiacae feles,
Have mercy on your flock.
Don't shred our brand new sofa
Or smash the Dresden clock.
Award us your epiphanies
Ablaze in morning light
And sit beside us purring
To guard us through the night.

FILM NOIR

It's a farm town in the August heat
With a couple of bars along Main Street.
A jukebox moans from an open door
Where a bored waiter sweeps the floor.

A bus pulls up by Imperial Fruit.
A guy gets off in a new prison suit.
He's not bad looking. Medium height.
Full of ambition. Not too bright.

He's a low life. He's one of the lost
Who's burnt every bridge he's ever crossed.
Just out of the slammer, a ticking bomb,
The Wrath of God and Kingdom Come.

It's the long odds on a roll of the dice
For big stakes you can't bet twice.
The cards get dealt. The wheel spins.
At the end of the night the house always wins.

He sees her alone at the end of the bar,
Smoking and hot like a fallen star.
She's a cold beauty with a knowing wink.
If she shot you dead, she'd finish your drink.

Some guys learn from their mistakes,
But all he learned is to raise the stakes.
There's something he forgot in jail—
That the female's deadlier than the male.

It's tough love from a hard, blue flame,
And you can't beat a pro at her own game.
It's the long con. It's the old switcheroo.
You think you're a player, but the mark is you.

She's married but lonely. She wishes she could.
Watch your hands! Oh, that feels good.
She whispers how much she needs a man.
If only he'd help her. She has a plan.

Their eyes meet, and he can tell
It's gonna be fun, but it won't end well.
He hears her plot with growing unease.
She strokes his cheek, and he agrees.

It's a straight shot. It's an easy kill.
If he doesn't help her, some other guy will.
It's a sleek piece with only one slug.
Spin the chambers and give it a tug.

The heat of her lips, the silk of her skin.
His body ignites. He pushes in.
They lie in the dark under the fan—
A sex-drunk chump, a girl with a plan.

· VII ·

LOVE

THANKS FOR REMEMBERING US

The flowers sent here by mistake,
signed with a name that no one knew,
are turning bad. What shall we do?
Our neighbor says they're not for her,
and no one has a birthday near.
We should thank someone for the blunder.
Is one of us having an affair?
At first we laugh, and then we wonder.

The iris was the first to die,
enshrouded in its sickly sweet
and lingering perfume. The roses
fell one petal at a time,
and now the ferns are turning dry.
The room smells like a funeral,
but there they sit, too much at home,
accusing us of some small crime,
like love forgotten, and we can't
throw out a gift we've never owned.

THE SUNDAY NEWS

Looking for something in the Sunday paper,
I flipped by accident to *Local Weddings,*
Yet missed the photograph until I saw
Your name among the headings.

And there you were, looking almost unchanged,
Your hair still long, though now long out of style,
And you still wore that stiff, ironic look
That was your smile.

I felt as though we sat there face to face.
My stomach tightened. I read the item through.
It said too much about both families,
Too little about you.

Finished at last, I put the paper down,
Stung by jealousy, my mind aflame—
Hating this man, this stranger whom you loved,
This printed name.

And yet I clipped it out to put away
Inside a book like something I might use,
A scrap I knew I wouldn't read again
But couldn't bear to lose.

SPEECH FROM A NOVELLA

Every night I wake and find myself
Alone in this strange bedroom. Always puzzled,
I walk into the hallway, blinking at the lights
And somehow know I'm on the highest floor
Of an enormous mansion full of people.
Then leaning on the banister I hear
The noise of a party down below,
And sad, slow music drifting up the stairwell
Like one last waltz that an exhausted band
Will play to satisfy an audience
That won't go home. Curious, I descend
The elegantly curving staircase, finding
Each floor darker and more crowded, people
Everywhere: on the landing, in the corridors,
Some staring, others arguing, most so drunk
They don't even notice that I'm there.

Then someone calls, "Mary, come down, come down,
And dance with us!" I try to answer him,
But it's so dark and crowded I can't see
The bottom yet, and I keep walking down
Until the music, laughter, cheap perfume,
The shouting people, all the smoke from cigarettes
Make me so dizzy I could faint, and still
He calls me, "Mary, come down, come down,"
And as I reach for him, the voices pause,
The music stops, and there is nothing there
But one voice laughing in another room.

SPEAKING OF LOVE

Speaking of love was difficult at first.
We groped for those lost, untarnished words
That parents never traded casually at home,
The radio had not devalued.
How little there seemed left to us.

So, speaking of love, we chose
The harsh and level language of denial
Knowing only what we did not wish to say,
Choosing silence in our terror of a lie.
For surely love existed before words.

But silence can become its own cliché,
And bodies lie as skillfully as words,
So one by one we spoke the easy lines
The other had resisted but desired,
Trusting that love renewed their innocence.

Was it then that words became unstuck?
That star no longer seemed enough for star?
Our borrowed speech demanded love so pure
And so beyond our power that we saw
How words were only forms of our regret.

And so at last we speak again of love,
Now that there is nothing left unsaid,
Surrendering our voices to the past,
Which has betrayed us. Each of us alone,
With no words left to summon back our love.

EQUATIONS OF THE LIGHT

Turning the corner, we discovered it
just as the old wrought-iron lamps went on—
a quiet, tree-lined street, only one block long
resting between the noisy avenues.

The streetlamps splashed the shadows of the leaves
across the whitewashed brick, and each tall window
glowing through the ivy-decked facade
promised lives as perfect as the light.

Walking beneath the trees, we counted all
the high black doors of houses bolted shut.
And yet we could have opened any door,
entered any room the evening offered.

Or were we so deluded by the strange
equations of the light, the vagrant wind
searching the trees, that we believed this brief
conjunction of our separate lives was real?

It seemed that moment lingered like a ghost,
a flicker in the air, smaller than a moth,
a curl of smoke flaring from a match,
haunting a world it could not touch or hear.

There should have been a greeting or a sign,
the smile of a stranger, something beyond
the soft refusals of the summer air
and children trading secrets on the steps.

Traffic bellowed from the avenue.
Our shadows moved across the street's long wall,
and at the end what else could we have done
but turn the corner back into our life?

THE VOYEUR

. . . and watching her undress across the room,
oblivious of him, watching as her slip
falls soundlessly and disappears in shadow,
and the dim lamplight makes her curving frame
seem momentarily both luminous
and insubstantial—like the shadow of a cloud
drifting across a hillside far away.

Watching her turn away, this slender ghost,
this silhouette of mystery, his wife,
walk naked to her bath, the room around her
so long familiar that it is, like him,
invisible to her, he sees himself
suspended in the branches by the window,
entering this strange bedroom with his eyes.

Seen from the darkness, even the walls glow—
a golden woman lights the amber air.
He looks and aches not only for her touch
but for the secret that her presence brings.
She is the moonlight, sovereign and detached.
He is a shadow flattened on the pavement,
the one whom locks and windows keep away.

But what he watches here is his own life.
He is the missing man, the loyal husband,
sitting in the room he craves to enter,
surrounded by the flesh and furniture of home.
He notices a cat curled on the bed.
He hears a woman singing in the shower.
The branches shake their dry leaves like alarms.

SPIDER IN THE CORNER

Cold afternoon: rain spattering the windows,
the dampness spreading slowly like a mold
in the poverty of gray November light.

Another day of books and spoiled plans,
of cigarettes and sitting still
in rooms too small for us. How little there

is left to talk about except the weather.
And so we tolerate the silence
like the spider in the corner neither one

of us will kill. Yes, the doorway whispers.
But we will stay—until the weather clears,
the endless rain that keeps us here together.

SUMMER STORM

We stood on the rented patio
While the party went on inside.
You knew the groom from college.
I was a friend of the bride.

We hugged the brownstone wall behind us
To keep our dress clothes dry
And watched the sudden summer storm
Floodlit against the sky.

The rain was like a waterfall
Of brilliant beaded light,
Cool and silent as the stars
The storm hid from the night.

To my surprise, you took my arm—
A gesture you didn't explain—
And we spoke in whispers, as if we two
Might imitate the rain.

Then suddenly the storm receded
As swiftly as it came.
The doors behind us opened up.
The hostess called your name.

I watched you merge into the group,
Aloof and yet polite.
We didn't speak another word
Except to say good-night.

Why does that evening's memory
Return with this night's storm—
A party twenty years ago,
Its disappointments warm?

There are so many *might-have-beens,*
What-ifs that won't stay buried,
Other cities, other jobs,
Strangers we might have married.

And memory insists on pining
For places it never went,
As if life would be happier
Just by being different.

THE LOST GARDEN

If ever we see those gardens again,
The summer will be gone—at least our summer.
Some other mockingbird will concertize
Among the mulberries, and other vines
Will climb the high brick wall to disappear.

How many footpaths crossed the old estate—
The gracious acreage of a grander age—
So many trees to kiss or argue under,
And greenery enough for any mood.
What pleasure to be sad in such surroundings.

At least in retrospect. For even sorrow
Seems bearable when studied at a distance,
And if we speak of private suffering,
The pain becomes part of a well-turned tale
Describing someone else who shares our name.

Still, thinking of you, I sometimes play a game.
What if we had walked a different path one day,
Would some small incident have nudged us elsewhere
The way a pebble tossed into a brook
Might change the course a hundred miles downstream?

The trick is making memory a blessing,
To learn by loss subtraction of desire,
Of wanting nothing more than what has been,
To know the past forever lost, yet seeing
Behind the wall a garden still in blossom.

BEING HAPPY

Of course it was doomed. I know that now,
but it ended so quickly, and I was young.
I hardly remember that summer in Seattle—
except for her. The city seems just a rainy backdrop.
From the moment I first saw her at the office
I was hooked. I started visiting her floor.

I couldn't work unless I caught a glimpse of her.
Once we exchanged glances, but we never spoke.
Then at a party we found ourselves alone.
We started kissing and ended up in bed.
We talked all night. She claimed she had liked me
secretly for months. I wonder now if that was true.

Two weeks later her father had a heart attack.
While she was in Chicago, they shut down our division.
I was never one for writing letters.
On the phone we had less to say each time.
And that was it—just those two breathless weeks,
then years of mild regret and intermittent speculation.

Being happy is mostly like that. You don't see it up close.
You recognize it later from the ache of memory.
And you can't recapture it. You only get to choose
whether to remember or forget, whether to feel remorse
or nothing at all. Maybe it wasn't really love.
But who can tell when nothing deeper ever came along?

THE PRESENT

The present that you gave me months ago
is still unopened by our bed,
sealed in its rich blue paper and bright bow.
I've even left the card unread
and kept the ribbon knotted tight.
Why needlessly unfold and bring to light
the elegant contrivances that hide
the costly secret waiting still inside?

THE LUNATIC, THE LOVER, AND THE POET

The tales we tell are either false or true,
But neither purpose is the point. We weave
The fabric of our own existence out of words,
And the right story tells us who we are.
Perhaps it is the words that summon us.
The tale is often wiser than the teller.
There is no naked truth but what we wear.

So let me bring this story to our bed.
The world, I say, depends upon a spell
Spoken each night by lovers unaware
Of their own sorcery. In innocence
Or agony the same words must be said,
Or the raging moon will darken in the sky.
The night grow still. The winds of dawn expire.

And if I'm wrong, it cannot be by much.
We know our own existence came from touch,
The new soul summoned into life by lust.
And love's shy tongue awakens in such fire—
Flesh against flesh and midnight whispering—
As if the only purpose of desire
Were to express its infinite unfolding.

And so, my love, we are two lunatics,
Secretaries to the wordless moon,
Lying awake, together or apart,
Transcribing every touch or aching absence
Into our endless, intimate palaver,
Body to body, naked to the night,
Appareled only in our utterance.

THE APPLE ORCHARD

You won't remember it—the apple orchard
We wandered through one April afternoon,
Climbing the hill behind the empty farm.

A city boy, I'd never seen a grove
Burst in full flower or breathed the bittersweet
Perfume of blossoms mingled with the dust.

A quarter mile of trees in fragrant rows
Arching above us. We walked the aisle,
Alone in spring's ephemeral cathedral.

We had the luck, if you can call it that,
Of having been in love but never lovers—
The bright flame burning, fed by pure desire.

Nothing consumed, such secrets brought to light!
There was a moment when I stood behind you,
Reached out to spin you toward me . . . but I stopped.

What more could I have wanted from that day?
Everything, of course. Perhaps that was the point—
To learn that what we will not grasp is lost.

COME BACK

Come back, come back to me—now that I'm old—
not love, but you, the shadow of love, fashioned
from quiet and quotidian things, glimpses
of rooftops, alleyways, of open windows
where lovers first espy the imminence
of their own loving, or from sickroom skylights
with their careworn parade of painful days,
the shadowy refuge that vanishes
the way a wild duck, shot in mid-flight,
drops suddenly to vanish in the marsh,
just a few feathers drifting in the air:
I am a shimmering reality
that has no purpose,
unless you return, love, shadow of love,
o cherished sleep, and grant me your repose.

(From the Italian of Carlo Betocchi)

AN OLD STORY

Our story is an old story, the tale of two,
Who met in our feverish, infallible youth
And woke transfigured in a world made new.

We walked through gardens of such stark perfume
That merely breathing left us drunk for days.
We rolled in brambles with our skin unbruised.

We shined in sunlight and in moonlight glowed,
As radiant as angels drawn by Blake.
How could such fiery brightness not explode?

The aspens shimmered, and each blade-like leaf
Slashed at the slopes until the freshets bled.
The mountains were not larger than our grief.

I don't know why I tell myself this story,
Except that it is spring again outside
When bent oaks briefly blossom into glory.

Oh, yes, it was a story beyond telling,
And so it had to end, as legend required
In blood and tears and fire, the grim fates smiling.

We had our years of ecstasy and rage,
And then moved back to other tamer tales.
But my hand still burns touching this page.

MARRIAGE OF MANY YEARS

Most of what happens happens beyond words.
The lexicon of lip and fingertip
defies translation into common speech.
I recognize the musk of your dark hair.
It always thrills me, though I can't describe it.
My finger on your thigh does not touch skin—
it touches *your* skin warming to my touch.
You are a language I have learned by heart.

This intimate patois will vanish with us,
its only native speakers. Does it matter?
Our tribal chants, our dances round the fire
performed the sorcery we most required.
They bound us in a spell time could not break.
Let the young vaunt their ecstasy. We keep
our tribe of two in sovereign secrecy.
What must be lost was never lost on us.

ACKNOWLEDGMENTS

The new poems in this collection, sometimes in slightly different versions, have appeared in the following journals: "An Old Story," "Come Back," "Monster," "Progress Report," and "Style" first appeared in the *Hudson Review;* "Household Gods," "Title Index to My Next Book of Poems," and "My Handsome Cousin" were published in *Radio Silence;* "Homage to Soren Kierkegaard" appeared in *First Things;* "Marriage of Many Years," "Sea Pebbles: An Elegy," and "Vultures Mating" were published in the *Sewanee Review;* and "Film Noir" and "Meditation on a Line from Novalis" first appeared in *Virginia Quarterly Review.* "Homecoming" is a revision of "The Homecoming" from *The Gods of Winter.* "Most Journeys Come to This" was originally published in *Daily Horoscope* under the title "Instructions for the Afternoon." "Film Noir," "My Handsome Cousin," and "Homage to Soren Kierkegaard" also appeared in limited editions by Aralia Press. Artichoke Editions printed a folio edition of "Sea Pebbles: An Elegy."

The author wishes to thank all of these editors and printers for their generous support.

NOTE ON THE TEXTS

The poems in this volume were selected from my first four collections supplemented by fifteen new poems, one of which is very long. *99 Poems* has been arranged by theme, not by chronology, because it is designed for the reader rather than the scholar. Within each section, however, the poems appear in chronological order with the new work at the end. The index lists the volumes in which the individual works originally appeared.

—*DG*

INDEX

Daily Horoscope (DH), 1986
The Gods of Winter (GW), 1991
Interrogations at Noon (IN), 2001
Pity the Beautiful (PB), 2012
New (*)

DANA GIOIA was born in Los Angeles in 1950. He received his B.A. and M.B.A. degrees from Stanford University. He also has an M.A. in Comparative Literature from Harvard University. For fifteen years he worked as a business executive in New York before quitting in 1992 to write full-time. He has published four earlier collections of poetry—*Daily Horoscope* (1986), *The Gods of Winter* (1991), *Interrogations at Noon* (2001) which won the American Book Award, and *Pity the Beautiful* (2012). Gioia's first critical collection, *Can Poetry Matter?* (1992), was a finalist for the National Book Critics Circle Award. He has received the Laetare Medal from Notre Dame University and the Aiken Taylor Award for lifetime contribution to American poetry. From 2003 to 2009 he served as Chairman of the National Endowment for the Arts. An essayist, reviewer, and translator, Gioia has also published fifteen anthologies of poetry and fiction. He divides his time between Los Angeles and Sonoma County, California. In 2011 he became the Judge Widney Professor of Poetry and Public Culture at the University of Southern California. In 2016 he was named California Poet Laureate.

The text of *99 Poems: New & Selected* is set in Galliard type
and was based on a design by Tree Swenson.
Composition by Bookmobile Design and Digital
Publisher Services, Minneapolis, Minnesota.
Manufactured by McNaughton & Gunn on acid-free,
100 percent postconsumer wastepaper.